THE
LEEDS YELLOW BOOK
2015

Essays on a

Liberal future for Leeds

Beecroft Publications
Leeds

The Leeds Yellow Book

Published in 2015 by
Beecroft Publications
72 Waterloo Lane
Bramley, Leeds
LS13 2JF
www.beecroftpublications.co.uk

A CIP catalogue record for this book is available from the
British Library

ISBN 978-0-9527025-9-7

Design and typography by Elizabeth Bee (c) 2015

Printed and bound in the Great Britain by CPI Group (UK) Ltd,
Croydon, CR0 4YY

The authors and editor are grateful to a number of subscribers who
have made this publication possible

CONTENTS

THE YELLOW BOOK

Liberal "Yellow Books" derive their title from the series of policy reports commissioned by David Lloyd George when he became leader of the united Liberal Party in October 1926. They were published for the 1929 General Election but, although they had a significant effect on public opinion and helped to add over two million votes to the Liberal total of the previous election in 1924, the party was still well down in third place in terms of MPs elected. The different reports such as on "The Land Question" and "Coal and Power" each had a different coloured cover. The most important one was on "Britain's Industrial Future" and had a yellow cover. It was henceforth referred to as the "Yellow Book." Much of it was written by John Maynard Keynes and a "popular" version was published under the title, "We can conquer unemployment."

A paragraph from this 1928 "Yellow Book" summed up the Liberals' overall approach:

> The measures we advocate for all these things spring from one clear purpose. We believe with a passionate faith that the end of all political and economic action is not the perfecting of this or that piece of mechanism or organisation but that individual men and women may have life and that they have it more abundantly.

All subsequent "Yellow Books", including this one, have this philosophy in mind.

FOREWORD

by Richard Brett

I am very pleased to have been asked to write a few words introducing this book of ideas. I have always welcomed new strategic thinking and new creative thinking and this book has both. The years from May 2010 until the present have been very difficult in Leeds and elsewhere as Liberal Democrats have struggled to come to terms with the implications for local elections of being a party of government.

The May 2014 elections were slightly more encouraging at Leeds City Council level in terms of winning seats but the Liberal Democrat base vote was very worrying and the European election results were disastrous. Now is very much the right time to search for new ideas and repackage older core themes.

The core themes which I am pleased to see running clearly through this book include making as many decisions about Leeds issues in Leeds with Leeds people empowered as much as possible. We need also to devolve decisions about each suburb or parish to groups in each area. Liberal Democrats equal Local Devolution.

I am also pleased to see the development of Leeds City Region (LCR) being addressed. While I was joint leader of Leeds City Council, LCR groups were formed for many topics and the City Region must be the future economic powerhouse which creates new jobs, better transport and improved strategic planning. I support developing Leeds City

Region and, just as an elected mayor for London allowed London to push forward major projects, I believe there should be an elected mayor for all ten council areas in the City Region to give it a better focus.

Though I do not necessarily support all the ideas and themes included, I absolutely recommend this book as a start of the fight back for Liberal ideas in Leeds. All serious campaigners, councillors and activists should read it and turn the best of the ideas into Liberal Democrat policy for Leeds.

Richard Brett
Councillor for Burmantofts and Richmond Hill Ward 2004–2011
Leader of the Leeds Liberal Democrat Group and joint leader of Council
2007–2010

INTRODUCTION

by Ian MacFadyen & Michael Meadowcroft

It may seem brave or foolhardy to publish a book of Liberal Democrat essays in the shadow of the worst election results the Liberal Democrat party has experienced. It is neither. It is an act of faith in a Liberal future for Europe, the United Kingdom and our great city of Leeds.

The Liberal Democrats will rebuild. Those of us who have been Liberals, Social Democrats and Liberal Democrats have rebuilt before and will do so again. We have begun already.

This book is part of the rebuilding. To win people's trust and confidence once more we have to offer clear visions of how our country and our city should be governed for all the people on Liberal Democrat values, principles and policies.

We offer fresh ideas. The United Kingdom needs fresh ideas. Leeds needs fresh ideas.

The Liberal Democrats have brought new thinking to national government through the coalition and have transformed the lives of millions by increasing the amount of our earnings we keep before we have to pay tax. Over three million people on low income will pay no tax at all thanks to the Liberal Democrats. So much more could be done to improve the lives of everyone if the Liberal Democrats formed a majority government.

We need a Liberal Democrat majority city government to make Leeds truly the place where regardless of their start in life, and circumstances since, everybody can get on and make things better for themselves, their families and their communities. The Liberal Democrat-led coalition council administration between 2004 and 2010 made a start and showed that Liberal Democrat city government works.

Liberal Democrats implemented equal pay for all council workers in Leeds, despite opposition on the council and a damaging strike, without workers having to go to the courts to secure their rights to pay justice. By contrast, in Birmingham the opponents prevailed, causing workers to go to court where they won, but now Birmingham has to sell much loved public buildings to raise millions of pounds to pay the workers' fair pay, court costs and other related bills.

The eclectic essays in this book have been written over the past year by new writers and seasoned writers as personal visions of how Liberal Democrats can transform Leeds.

In writing, we argue for strengthened local government and for strengthened communities, where everyone, whatever their ethnicity, religion, level of ability or disability, family circumstances or sexual orientation, can get on together and fulfil their potential individually and collectively. We want education to give life chances to young people in their communities and we want communities to be able to offer alternatives that will help young and not-so-young people avoid or turn from crime and anti-social behaviour. Culture, especially your culture, should be nurtured without dulling its vitality. People should be freed and enabled to regenerate the economy of Leeds and the Leeds City Region. Transport and infrastructure is challenging and only now, thanks to Liberal Democrats in government, is the city and region being equipped with the necessary powers and funding, but more is needed. For a healthy city where health and life chances are equal, regardless of birth circumstances, social status and income, we need new ideas and we need to explore the use of social media in public health.

We wanted to produce a book of essays that demonstrated more intellectual rigour than is, alas, usual in politics today. So this is not a manifesto: these are the personal analyses and ideas of each author, not necessarily policies of the Liberal Democrat party, but we hope they will contribute to the development of Leeds Liberal Democrat manifestos year on year. In particular, we hope that the ideas here, and the picture they paint of a Liberal society in Leeds will encourage you to join the challenge of making them happen. Do please contact us with your comments and questions.

We thank Vitus Asaga Bawa, Joanne Binns, Ryk Downes, Anthony Lockett and Ruth Péchèr for their chapters and Elizabeth Bee for her editing.

Unless indicated otherwise, figures quoted are as of autumn 2013.

– 1 –

LEEDS & ITS REGION

Leeds, people, council and region: a profile

by Ian MacFadyen

Liberal Democrats want to end poverty and bring prosperity for all the people. Liberal Democrats believe in unlocking the dynamic potential of local areas. For too long local government has been simply the agent of central government, confined by tight budgetary controls and made cautious beyond due diligence by legislation whose extent and complexity ensures inaction is often safer than action. Liberal Democrats, therefore, look for ways to set local authorities free for innovation to burgeon. Through the City Deal agreed with central government, powers are being devolved to Leeds and the Leeds City Region (and other City Regions). The test for this City Deal is whether Leeds and the City Region is genuinely empowered and freed, or whether the reality will be a new form of control by Whitehall. The challenge for Liberal Democrats in Leeds and throughout the City Region is to use this opportunity to offer and secure a mandate for a Liberal Democrat Leeds City Region in which everyone's life is improved through Liberalism.

Change

Local government exists to fulfil duties – that is, provide certain services, collect council taxes and some other revenues and regulate particular activities – and to exercise the new General Power of Competence and other powers set out in acts of parliament. The General Power of Competence and City Deals are innovations by which local government is undergoing profound bespoke changes, rather than undergoing uniform changes regardless of local circumstances. It is significant that at cabinet level in the coalition the minister leading this initiative is Nick Clegg, the Liberal Democrat leader and Deputy Prime Minister.[1]

Who lives in Leeds and the Leeds City Region?

The 2011 census[2] found 751,485 people – 51% of them female – living in Leeds, making Leeds the third largest local authority by population in the United Kingdom after London and Birmingham and larger than two member states of the European Union, Luxembourg and Malta. Eighteen per cent of Leeds' population are children and 15% are aged 65 or over. The combined population of the ten-authority Leeds City Region is 2,952,057,[3] greater than the populations of Northern Ireland and six European Union member states.

The population increase since the 2001 census was 5% in Leeds which is lower than elsewhere: 6% was the average for Yorkshire and the Humber and 7% for England and Wales.

Eighty eight percent of people in Leeds were born in the UK. The 12% born outside the UK is higher than ten years previously, when the figure was 7%. Over two-thirds of those born outside the UK were born outside the EU. Of those living in Leeds, according to the census, 85% are white. Fifteen per cent are non-white, up from ten years earlier and slightly higher than the average for England and Wales. At 3% (22,500) the Pakistani community is the largest Black and Minority Ethnic group, with Indians and Africans next with about 2% each. English is the main language in 92% of households, but 4.5% of households have no-one speaking English as a main language. Fewer people in Leeds say they are Christian than in England and Wales as a whole, while higher proportions say they Jewish, Muslim or Sikh.

Serving the people

Leeds City Council comprises 99 councillors elected in 33 wards. Ten are currently Liberal Democrats, 63 Labour, 18 Conservative, five

Morley Borough Independents, two Green Party, and one Independent, who was elected as a Conservative in 2011. Turnout across the city in 2014 was 34.56%.[4]

The city has a cabinet form of administration, with an Executive Board, chaired by the leader of the council, who is the leader of the largest party, chosen by the councillors of that party. The Executive Board has (in 2014) eight portfolio-holding members covering: finance and inequality; children and families; neighbourhoods, planning and personnel; digital and creative technologies, culture and skills; transport and the economy; cleaner, stronger and safer communities; adult social care; health and wellbeing. The leaders of the Liberal Democrat and the Conservative councillors' groups are also members of the Executive Board. The Board has eleven meetings a year.[5]

The full 99 member council meets seven times a year. It approves the budget and council plan, elects the Lord Mayor and Deputy Lord Mayor, receives deputations, receives reports from the Executive Board and other boards and committees, holds question time, considers motions proposed by councillors and other statutory duties.

Much decision making is delegated to committees, for example, Area Committees, the Corporate Governance and Audit Committee, and the Standards and Conduct Committee. Scrutiny Boards review particular services and make recommendations, and can call-in decisions by the Executive Board and other committees for review before they are implemented.[6]

The Leeds City Council constitution, agreed by the Council, "Sets out how the Council operates, how decisions are made and the procedures which are followed to ensure that these are efficient, transparent and accountable to local people. Some of these processes are required by law, while others are a matter for the Council to choose".[7] It sets out powers delegated to officers to act and take decisions on behalf of the Executive Board.

Leeds City Council, how it got to be so

Leeds in its current size and boundaries was created by the Local Government Act 1972, which established the metropolitan district of Leeds, incorporating the former county borough of Leeds with the boroughs and urban districts of Aireborough, Garforth, Horsforth, Morley, Otley, Pudsey, Rothwell, and parts of Tadcaster, Wetherby and Wharfedale districts. Leeds received a Royal Charter as a city in 1893 and this city status applies to the whole metropolitan district. Its original borough charter dates back to 1626 and its first public election was in 1835.

The 1972 act abolished the West Riding County Council, which extended from Sheffield in the south to Sedburgh in the north, and replaced it with the metropolitan counties of West Yorkshire and South Yorkshire and placed some areas into other counties. The metropolitan counties were abolished by the Local Government Act 1985, when Leeds City Council then became a unitary authority.

Large as the council currently is, it is not the largest it has been. In 1968, the county borough of Leeds was smaller in area than present day Leeds, but the council had 120 members from 30 wards – 90 councillors and 30 aldermen. Aldermen on councils were abolished in 1974, but the title is retained as an honour councils can bestow.

Combined authorities: collaboration

Formed in 2004,[8] the Leeds City Region comprises Barnsley, Bradford, Calderdale, Craven, Harrogate, Kirklees, Leeds, Selby, Wakefield and York. Councillors from authorities in the City Region, together with representatives of the private sector and higher education form a local enterprise partnership, the largest outside London. The Leeds City Region Enterprise Partnership negotiated the City Deal with central government. Under the City Deal[9] (covered in more detail in chapter 7) the City Region gains powers to create a self-sustaining economic investment fund, to tackle youth unemployment, to develop transport and broadband and a low carbon economy. In return, the councils in the City Region have set up a new transport and economic prosperity combined authority to replace Metro, the West Yorkshire Integrated Transport Authority (which is covered by Ryk Downes in chapter 4). It involves the Metro authorities first, with the other councils in the City Region joining the combined authority in ways that fit their differing legal responsibilities as unitary or district authorities. The first such combined authority was the Greater Manchester Combined Authority, established on 1 April 2011, whose membership is one councillor nominated by each member council, rather than by direct election by voters.[10] Leeds City Council also collaborates with other councils for procurement, through the Yorkshire Purchasing Organisation,[11] and in other ways.

The General Power of Competence
Since February 2012 local authorities have, under the Localism Act, the General Power of Competence to do anything that an individual can do that is not specifically prohibited.[12] Previously, local authorities could only do what the law said they could do. There is no requirement to consider whether any economic, social or environmental well-being will result as there was with local authorities' previous wide powers. While this is a broad new power, it does not entitle councils to do anything they think fit. It does not empower them, for example, to impose new taxes, because individual citizens have no power to tax.[13] Nor does it enable local authorities to get round restrictions on the use of powers that existed before the Localism Act to do things that were expressly prevented or limited before the General Power of Competence was available, or do anything that might be prevented or limited by Parliament after the Localism Act was passed.

With its 241 sections and 25 schedules – implemented by, up to mid August 2014, 17 pieces of subordinate legislation for England (and others for Wales and Greater London) – the Localism Act[14] also gives councils more powers to offer discounts on business rates, obliges local authorities to put to local referenda council tax rises above levels approved by Parliament and gives local communities rights to bid for assets of community value. There are also changes to planning and housing rules. The Standards Board for England is replaced by codes to be drawn up by councils and an offence is created of failing to declare or of misrepresenting a financial interest.

Liberal Democrat ministers led work to enact the General Power of Competence, although it was not a commitment in the Liberal Democrat manifesto for 2010 general election. It was in the Conservative manifesto and was included in "The Coalition: our programme for government" (the coalition agreement).[15] In 2010, before the general election, the Local Government Association sponsored a Local Government (Power of General Competence) Bill in Parliament. Neither before this bill, nor in the bill that became the Localism Act, does there seem to have been any assessment of gaps or defects in existing powers that the General Power of Competence would remedy. Liberal Democrat councillors are said to have mixed views on the General Power of Competence and the Act as a whole. It is considered a useful tool, but councils have to take time to check whether any planned actions were prevented or limited before or after the Localism Act. Doing this has on occasion revealed specific powers to use instead of the General Power of Competence. As yet there are few examples of the General Power of Competence being used. Its breadth might lead to issues about holding councillors to account.[16]

The City Region combined authority will have a wide power of competence in carrying out its functions, but not the General Power of Competence available to an individual local authority.

Polity

It is not clear that these changes have a ballot box mandate from the people of Leeds and the City Region, although the Leeds City Region Leaders' Board was formally established as a statutory joint committee in 2007 and meets in public and the process of establishing the new combined authority has required full council agreement in each of the local authorities.

Councillors are their constituents' advocates with the council and its arm's length bodies. On constituents' behalf they ensure obligations are fulfilled, such as filling potholes or making repairs in social housing, they oppose developments or other changes and hold those in authority in the council and certain other public bodies to account in council debates and committee work. This is the pattern of the Liberal Democrats' community politics.

Leeds's electoral practice of electing one third of the council each year for three years and then having a year with no election (the year which previously saw the county council election) works well, offering the opportunity – if not the reality – of continuous renewal. But this pattern of elections provides no point at which all prospective elected members of the Leeds City Council present their own or their party's short, medium and long-term plans to receive a mandate and give account to the voters for mandates already given. Making changes, producing proposals, securing council and parliamentary approval, and carrying out what has been agreed takes a number of years and relies on appropriate relationships of accountability between officers (as the civil service of local government) and elected members. All this requires clear mandates from the people given at elections when the people can hold councillors to account for their use of their mandate. Instead, elections by thirds enable parties to assume and interpret mandates.

An elected mayor would have resolved this dilemma by being a democratic office based on seeking and receiving such mandates for change, without diluting elections based on councillors' traditional role. The Liberal Democrat elected mayor in Watford has been a success, winning re-election with increased majorities twice. In Bedford, a Liberal Democrat was elected mayor in a by-election in 2009 and re-elected with an increased majority in 2011. In the opinion of this writer, it was a mistake of Leeds Liberal Democrats to oppose the creation of an elected mayor for Leeds and regrettable that in the referendum in 2012 voters rejected the proposal.

Another solution is needed and it is suggested, first, that the pattern of elections should be changed to the election of the full council every four years. Second, alongside their candidates in each ward, parties should be able to present their leaders for the voters' endorsement as prospective Leaders of the Council, rather than, as now, presenting these people only in the wards where they stand, with little if any presentation of them as leaders in the rest of the city. Leeds would then have a municipal general election, which could give a mandate and the time to carry it out, without the uncertainty of annual one-third elections, but with an endorsement by the voters of the Leader of the Council.

Making the case, winning a mandate

On their own, these changes would not necessarily ensure mandates from the people, because, despite the size of Leeds compared with other parts of the United Kingdom and the European Union, elections are not fought on alternative visions and programmes to best promote the welfare and prosperity of the people of Leeds. Instead, elections are only fought on candidates' merits as advocates and their opposition to developments and changes. This denies the people of Leeds the chance in elections to set a course for their own and their city's future. It leaves the administration without a mandate. It means the City Deal, which could have been put to the people as a work in progress at the last city council elections, lacks the popular mandate that can only be given by the people of Leeds and the Leeds City Region in an election.

Leeds Liberal Democrats published their programmes in council election manifestos in 2010 and 2011, but other parties did not respond with their own and there were no debates. Moreover, most Liberal Democrat candidates, like those of other parties, fought their elections on the basis of casework done, opposition to local developments, track records and sending stern rebukes to the coalition government.

For the new decentralised dispensation with enhanced powers for the city and the City Region, a different approach is needed. Parish pump politics in a city and City Region matching nation states in size cannot be the only approach to politics and to seeking election.

At each election parties should set out and debate: their values and achievable visions for the city; how they will improve life for all citizens and banish poverty; how they will use the city council's General Power of Competence and other powers; how they will carry out and develop the City Deal and other agreements; and what they will seek from central government in further negotiations. All this should be discussed and debated on every street, stair well, pub and café, community hall, club, bus stop, water cooler, Job Centre queue and everywhere else people meet; and the political parties should debate their plans with each other in every part of the city and City Region. This should be done throughout the ten local authorities in the Leeds City Region.

Liberal Democrats should continue to show the way by presenting their values and achievable vision in manifestos, leaflets, web sites, Facebook, Twitter, interviews and in every other way possible. Liberal Democrats should debate their vision with the public, so that elections become for something and not just against things. If the other parties will not debate, Liberal Democrats should expose their timidity and press on winning the public for a Liberal Democrat Leeds.

Endpiece
What is being described is the beginning of city government for Leeds, which in size and economy (as we show in a separate chapter) is a significant European city from which poverty in all its forms and for all ages should be banished. The challenge for Liberal Democrats in the Leeds City Region is to use the City Deal and other changes to achieve this end.

This chapter recommends: changing the pattern of elections to the election of the full council every four years; that in Leeds and throughout the Leeds City Region parties should present their leaders for the voters' endorsement as prospective Leaders of the Council; at each election parties should set out and debate their values and achievable visions of the city; and Liberal Democrats should continue to show the way by present their values and achievable vision in every way possible.

Bibliography

1. Cabinet Office, *Deputy Prime Minister launches more 'City Deals'*, [News release], 2013
2. Office for National Statistics/Leeds City Council, *Leeds - The Big Picture: A summary of the results of the 2011 Census,* [Online], 2012
3. Office for National Statistics, *2011 Census: Usual resident population by local authority,* [Online], 2012
4. Leeds City Council, *Leeds City Council Election Results 2012 & 2014,* [Online], 2012 & 2014
5. Leeds City Council, *Committee Details Executive Board,* [Online], 2012
6. Leeds City Council, *Council, Committees and Boards,* [Online], 2013
7. Leeds City Council, *Leeds City Council Constitution,* [Online], 2013
8. Leeds City Region, *Proposal: A Leeds City Region Deal,* Leeds, 2012
9. Cabinet Office, *Unlocking growth in cities: city deals – wave 1,* London 2012
10. Wikipedia, *Greater Manchester Combined Authority,* [Online], 2013
11. Dept. of the Environment, Transport and the Regions, MacFadyen I, *Buying Consortia,* London, 2001
12. *The Localism Act 2011 (Commencement No 3) Order 2012, SI 2012 No 411,* [Online]
13. Dept. for Communities and Local Government, *A plain English guide to the Localism Act,* London, 2011
14. *The Localism Act,* HMSO, 2011
15. Cabinet Office, *Coalition Programme for Government,* London, 2010
16. Local Government Association, *The General Power of Competence: Empowering councils to make a difference and Annex: case studies on how councils are using the General Power of Competence to bring about change and innovation,* London, 2013

CHILDREN

Where have all the children gone?????

by Joanne Binns

WHO'S THAT NOW??? GO ANSWER IT, STACEY, PLEASE.' Stacey went to the door.

'MUM!!' shouted Stacey up the hallway.

'WHAT?' I replied, getting up off the sofa.

'IT'S THE POLICE ANTI-SOCIAL BEHAVIOUR WOMAN,' she replied, while running upstairs.

I walked down the hallway puzzled, thinking, What have they done now?

'Hi, can I help you?' I asked abruptly.

'Yes. We have had complaints about Stacey and her friends hanging about the streets causing nuisance,' the anti-social behaviour officer, a Police Community Support Officer, replied while handing me a letter.

'Well there is nothing for them to do. They can't go to the community centre. All the rogues are there,' I replied very angrily.

'If you don't comply with the letter, you will be brought up before housing' replied the PCSO.

'OK, I will keep her in,' I replied, slamming the door in their faces.

I was so angry. I remember when kids could be kids. We used to play in our street, but now there are loads of "no ball games" signs all over. What happened to kerby, pegs, kick ball and hop it? I remember playing with my chopper bike and leaving it in the street for my friends to play on while I went in for my tea. When you came out it was still there. Now you can't even leave it in your own home, unless your house is like a prison with bars on doors and windows.

Days passed. Stacey played upstairs doing girly things, dressing up and messing about in her bedroom with her mates.

I was sitting chatting with my friend, when Stacey came down with her friends. 'Watch this.'

So I picked up my cuppa and got ready. Stacey and her friends did a little play. But it shocked me and my friend – talent here and going to waste. So we decided to start Drama Teens in my front room. Stacey wrote the script. I went with my friend round to the shop to try to get some things donated, but he offered discount on what we bought. Couldn't complain, every bit helps.

Three children became 17. I changed my room round to adapt to the growing numbers of children wanting to attend. My friend and I were on benefits and were struggling with money to keep Drama Teens going. We couldn't stop the group though. The children were having so much fun and really enjoying themselves. It was nice to see the kids who used to bully my son in a different light, children being children.

My friend got a leaflet through the door saying the church was holding an event, "Be safe in your home". We walked round collecting freebies from stalls to give to the children and keep ourselves. Also we talked and talked about what we were doing. We got asked to come and join the Unity Group at the community centre. My friend and I weren't happy to do that, but we had to do it for legal reasons, which we didn't know about, because we went into this blind. Who would have known that twelve months later my family's lives would be turned up side down.

A member of the estate didn't like the fact that I was building bridges between police and agencies with the children. Overnight things changed. A hate campaign started, if you can call it that. I called it a year of hell.

Children started throwing stones and eggs at my window, disrupting drama classes. My son, who has learning disabilities, was bullied and assaulted on a number of occasions. My daughter had a knife held to her throat. I was punched in the stomach when I was eight months pregnant.

One evening, a week after I had given birth to my baby boy, a bush outside my home was set on fire next to my gas meter. I was only made aware of this by a neighbour. I was scared for our lives. The neighbour stated she didn't recognise the youths. I felt very lonely as my neighbours were witnesses to the intimidation and harassment I received, but would not come forward with information due to fear of reprisals.

The nuisance didn't stop there. My number was put on buses, bus stops and on the internet. My daughter and I got some disgusting phone calls that I won't repeat. Some children even turned up at my daughter's school and intimidated her there.

In addition to the above problems, my children's father died, whilst we were subject to all this nuisance. We were trying to grieve, but were still subjected to abuse, including abusive text messages such has "Your mum's going to end up like your dad and so is your baby brother".

The day before their father was buried Social Security turned up at my door saying they had reason to believe that I was living with the children's father and that I was working. I informed them that the next day I was burying him. I was sure the youths were responsible for this. I was unable to prove it, but due to the actions of these local youths I had been driven to think this way, always having to look over my shoulder.

The effect of this anti-social behaviour on my family was devastating. My daughter wrote me a letter saying she wanted to kill herself. She could no longer cope. No longer safe walking to local shops, to the bus stop, to school, we didn't even feel safe sitting in our garden. We spent the summer months locked away.

So the final outcome of this is that out of 23 children and some adults, the courts awarded six full anti-social behaviour orders – ASBOs – to six main key youths. I had to attend court on six separate occasions, including the crown court, as one of the youths appealed the ASBO. I was hoping we would get a fresh start, but no, we had to relive the nightmares. The young person won his appeal, sadly. This young person, along with others, had driven us out of our home and made our lives misery.

Since that year of hell, I have founded the Forgotten Children's Foundation, www.freewebs.com/theforgottenchildrensfoundation.

In 2007, I won the Yorkshire Women of Achievement Award, overall, winner and the Jane Tomlinson Award. Also, I won the Respect Award. But my greatest reward was to be helping Safer Leeds to make changes so this sort of thing doesn't happen to anyone else, for example, by getting alley gates put up.

Now Leeds has an anti-social behaviour team of police, fire, victim support, housing, working together in one office, which helps with communication, not like what happended to me. I had to repeat myself to so many different people. Also, I am going into schools, educating parents and children. Just telling my story helps victims stand up and say, "No", or gets parents thinking about what their children are up to. It also shows the effect of the anti-social behaviour team.

There is loads more I have done. I could go on forever. The best things I've done are the trips for the forgotten children. They have helped the children reconnect, to have a family and have stopped families from being prisoners in their homes, but the best things were the smiles on the children's faces and the big hugs and thanks I received – amazing and so warming.

Most organisations champion equal opportunities and every child matters. This means being responsive to a young person's needs and also proactive by reaching out to young people to ensure that they have access to help and services. We are all aware this isn't always the case. Behind each family subjected to crime or anti-social behaviour there are the forgotten children.

There are many reactions to being victimised. Each young person's reaction is unique. Without help some young people may develop long term problems. A survey by the Howard League in 2008 found that 95% of children have been victims of crime at least once.

Research also highlights a vicious circle of crime, whereby an experience of being victimised at the age of 12 becomes a powerful indicator of offending at 15 years. There is also a significant overlap with at least as many young people both committing crimes and been victimised as those who are simply offending. This is why we need equal opportunities for victims. Stop the choice of staying in or joining in. Help build self esteem. Offer positive choices and healthy living. Young people don't receive a lot of help unlike perpetrators.

Liberals don't have a magic wand, but making the small changes to our communities helps make the big changes. "The Liberal Democrats exist," as the constitution says, "to build and safeguard a fair, free and open society, in which we balance the fundamental values of liberty, equality and community and in which no-one shall be enslaved by poverty, ignorance or conformity".

Giving communities a voice helps bring that community spirit what was once alive in our communities. We have to lay a path for our young people to follow. Promoting fun time isn't a crime. It's Liberal.

– 3 –

EDUCATION

The trials and tribulations of Leeds schools and Gove's legacy

by Michael Meadowcroft & Ruth Péchèr

The fate of education under the Labour Government of 1997, followed structurally along similar paths by the Coalition Government of 2010, has been the latest way of undermining local government. In Leeds, following the government taking powers over local education provision in 2001, the City Council lost control of its major financial responsibility for ten years, until it was able to take back control of the service in 2011. With the city's housing provision also being brought back into the City Council on 1 October 2013, after six years being run by "Arms Length Management Organisations", the elected authority once again had control of two of its most sensitive services.

Nevertheless, despite this regaining of powers, the City Council is not a free agent within the educational field. The personal powers of the Secretary of State detract from local democracy when regulation and the imposition of detailed rules, imposing the style and performance of schools, ceases to be a legitimate subject for debate and decision by elected councillors.

There is an urgent need to restore to the City Council the power to determine local education policies within a holistic provision of services to its citizens. The atomisation of provision is a highly retrograde step taking us back before 1902 when the separate School Board was brought within the ambit of the City Council.

Labour's policy is even more bizarre than was Michael Gove's. David Blunkett and Tristram Hunt apparently propose to establish a network of commissioners as "independent directors of school standards" in each city or group of local authorities.[1] The individuals are to be selected from a "list approved by the secretary of state" – a real recipe for partisan selection on the "one of us" syndrome. Simon Jenkins was scathing in *The Guardian*:

> "This is mystifying. Why not just return Whitehall's schools to elected local education authorities? These exist. They offer a tried and tested model for local accountability. ... I cannot see [Blunkett's] new commissioners as different in function or power from Gove's new chancellors. Indeed, it looks suspiciously as if government and opposition have been in cahoots on this. Gove should be quietly pleased.

> Real accountable delegation downwards of any local service can only be to elected people – as in most democracies around the world. They need to have proper local tax-raising and distributing powers to match. It is clear that Blunkett and Hunt can no more stomach this than could Cameron and Gove. Labour's hatred for localism, and especially elected localism, is as visceral as that of the Tories."[2]

For Liberals, democracy is crucially local democracy and nowhere is it more needed – with the opportunity for a co-ordinated approach to children's services that comes with it – than in education.

History
The key MP associated with educational reform in England was W E Forster,[3] a Liberal of Quaker origins and a long term Member for Bradford. His 1870 Elementary Education Act inaugurated elected school boards who had to make provision for the education of children between five and thirteen, though school attendance did not become compulsory until ten years later.

It is fair to say that for some one hundred and twenty years from Forster's Act to the central imposition of a national curriculum in 1988, education provision continued on "progressive" lines with policy in the hands of top-tier local authorities whose diversity ensured innovation and the evaluation of different ideas. Certainly differing educational theories and their outcomes were keenly debated – comprehensive versus grammar school provision, for instance – but during all that time there was no real pressure for a rigid uniform national policy and certainly no agitation for a national state directed curriculum, indeed the situation in France where it was said, wrongly as it happened, that it was possible to state what every French child was studying at every moment of the day, was ridiculed.

Within this devolved system, powerful chief education officers arose, including in our region Dr James Graham[4] in Leeds, CEO for twenty-four years, and Sir Alec Clegg,[5] the West Riding's CEO for almost thirty years, and they had considerable influence on the style and type of provision in their local authorities.

What is more, there was a substantial degree of consensus on educational provision across the parties. In Leeds it was Councillor Josh Walsh, Labour chair of the Leeds education committee for twenty-two years, who introduced the first comprehensive school, in Seacroft, in 1956 with three others following by 1967, when the Conservatives gained control of the City Council. However, the new education chair, Patrick Crotty, was also an enthusiast for the comprehensive principle and introduced a three-tier system (5–9, 9–13 and 13–18) across the whole city by 1972. Of all people, it was Margaret Thatcher who signed the order for the Leeds system when she became Secretary of State for Education in 1970. Paddy Crotty recounted that he was concerned that some members of his Conservative group, given the new Conservative Government, would renege on the comprehensive policy that he had struggled to get through and to finance. He knew that he would have to get the order signed by the Minister before his Conservative Group meeting on the Monday evening before Wednesday's City Council meeting. He therefore went personally to London on the Monday and virtually camped out in Mrs Thatcher's office until she signed! He then rushed back to Leeds with the policy irrevocable!

This broadly non-ideological approach locally was not seriously challenged and it was only the advent of ideological driven national politicians that undermined it. The initial central government "interference" came from Kenneth Baker as Secretary of State for Education in 1987 when he drove through the power for the Minister to enforce a national curriculum as part of the Education Reform Act 1988. Not only did Liberals, as the party of pluralism and of broad concepts of the purpose of education, not make the obvious objections to the policy, but even claimed that they had thought of it first! Incidentally, although described as a "national" curriculum, it did not apply to independent schools and, later, academies were to have a significant degree of autonomy to opt out.

Alongside the national curriculum came national testing of children at the ages of seven, eleven and fourteen, with published league tables of results. All this is deeply illiberal. Education is not primarily an issue of "teaching to examination" or to be confined to narrowly academic subjects, important though they certainly are. The problem is that there was too complacent a belief in an inexorable incremental progress and there was no real attempt to win public hearts and minds for concepts of education that were concerned with the whole personality and capability of each student. Consequently when Kenneth Baker held out the prospect of concentration on "basics" and the achievement of a certificate showing examination success, his backwoodsmanship found all too ready a popular resonance. The failure lies with Liberals and others who failed to persuade parents of what real education could mean for their children.

League tables now contain over 400 variables of school function but the main verdict of five GCSEs at A* to C remains the key factor in determining a school's position in the league. This is an over simplistic judgment in the analysis of a school's efficacy. Many schools offer specialised benefits to pupils which are hard to demonstrate in figures and data. For example, City of Leeds School, now the Leeds City Academy, has a highly successful English as an Additional Language Department catering to the more than three-quarters of the student population who do not have English as a mother tongue. The school has also been awarded School of Sanctuary status in recognition of its commitment to being a safe and welcoming place for those whose lives were in danger in their own country, who have troubles at home or are just looking for a space of safety.

The next step in undermining liberal education values came in 2000 with Labour's education advisor, Lord Adonis, promoting the opportunity for individual schools to opt out of local authority control and become "Academies". In a number of cases, including in Leeds, financial pressure was brought to bear to force local authority schools to opt out. Each academy is independent of the local authority but funded directly by the government, often with additional funding from individuals and organisations with an ideological axe to grind. The pressure for schools to become academies was personified by Michael Gove in the coalition government and as yet shows no sign of being abandoned by his successor, Nicky Morgan.

The final ideological way of potentially undermining progressive education came with the promotion of free schools, with significant funding from the government. Free schools do not have to be reactionary, as the example of A S Neill's Summerhill School,[6] established in 1921 and now run by his daughter, shows, but under Michael Gove's regime they were more likely to have an emphasis on discipline and a relatively narrow curriculum.

The promise of free schools was to narrow the gap between richer and poorer pupils by increasing the choice of education in all areas and, by virtue of a freer market, drive an improvement in educational standards. Regardless of the desirability or otherwise of applying an economic ethos to an essential children's service, there is some evidence, although disputed from central government, that free schools are more prevalent in wealthier areas and that free schools admit far less pupils on free school meals, the widely used indicator of a lower household income, than the national average.

This said, there have been some positive results of the free school initiative. Local residents may identify a need for local children that is not being met by current provision. The very first free special school in the country was opened in Leeds. The bid made to open a school offering a specialised curriculum and methodology for children and young people with an autistic spectrum condition was made by a group of parents who had experienced a gap in the provision offered to their children by Education Leeds. Their proposal was scrutinised by the Department of Education and opened as The Lighthouse School in September 2012.

Liberal values

Michael Gove's incessant concentration on structures and constitutions successfully diverted attention away from the far more important focus on the nature of education and on the purposes for which we educate our children. Liberals have had to fight urgent rearguard actions against each new educational atrocity and this has diverted us away from defending the essentials of education and promoting educational provisions which develop each child's potential. In particular, largely by default, parents have largely imbibed the Conservative notion that the aim and purpose of education is to enable students to pass exams and to acquire certificates indicating this ability.

This narrow perception of education, with its league tables that are devastating to many schools and teachers, has led to parents resorting to extreme measures to qualify for getting their children into schools high up the league table, or even to scraping together significant fees to do what they believe to be their duty for their children. Local authorities have paid millions of pounds each year to transport children across their area to schools often miles away from their homes because few parents in "downtown" areas, even those who hold on to a liberal perception of education, dare take the risk of not sending their children to schools with high examination attainments.

Another ubiquitous and all too pervasively accepted tenet of Thatcherism, which greatly affects the educational debate, is the denigration of the public service. The idea that private is good and that state is bad is a pernicious and, in its intellectual superficiality, a largely unchallenged belief in any rigorous way.

Even in its crudest form, the idea that the minority who are potentially high academic achievers should be promoted even if it has to be at the expense of the majority, has serious consequences for the community as a whole. That majority does not disappear, their schools are not closed, their teachers are not demoted and their parents are not silenced. But there is nothing worse than being disparaged and written off. It is a key Liberal value that every child, indeed every citizen, is worthy of respect and encouragement. An inability to solve quadratic equations or to parse sentences does not mean that one cannot be good neighbour, worker, parent or contributor to society. Only if a child or, particularly, an adolescent goes through the community school can he or she be expected to be sensitive to the needs of the community and to understand the breadth of levels of potential achievement. Separating children at the school gate is damaging to all concerned.

Many troublesome young people see little point in making an effort academically or cooperating socially at school often due to a history of failure or a perception that they have no hope of making a positive contribution to society or achieving economic well-being. Teachers must instil hope and aspiration for a bright future in this generation of young people but they must be provided with the necessary time and sympathetic support which encourages their energy and inspiration. Smaller schools and smaller classes are required that are streamed to allow teachers to target the specific needs of each learning group.

High school teachers whose classes are made up of up to 30 children may teach upwards of 200 pupils a week. This leaves little or no time to create relationships with each young person, not to mention the unmanageable amount of administration and marking that this entails, demoralising teachers and taking away their enthusiasm and professional vigour.

Not only is there a need to emphasise all those human values, such as music, drama, sport and civics that fall outside the narrow range of subjects that was the mark of Gove's system, but there are great values in having the holistic approach that the local authority strove to provide. Having the immediate availability of social services and housing departments is a considerable underpinning of support for children struggling to thrive in school. Even within the education service itself the range of support available is restricted by each individual school's budget constraints once they opt out into academies or are "free schools". Michael recalls, as a member of the Leeds education authority, spending many Friday afternoons, together with headteachers, advisors and welfare officers, finding solutions for persistent truants and their parents. The government let Gove divert this practical alternative and this multi-disciplinary child-centred approach into a zero tolerance policy to school absence that results in fines for parents whose children do not attend school. This fails to solve the underlying cause of the absence, risks causing financial hardship to families in need and damages a fragile home-school relationship still further.

Under local authority control, there were considerable support services available to assist teachers who were having difficulties in the classroom. Now, the denigration of the teaching profession that was a leitmotiv of the Gove regime shows no sign of being abandoned. Teachers are increasingly down-hearted and demotivated as a result of pressure from school leadership to produce results with disrespectful and disruptive behaviour in the classroom and a continuous negative mantra from the secretary of education that undermines teachers' esteem in the community. Teacher training is brief and teachers that seek to develop professionally with further qualifications find they are not routinely recognised or valued. With the increasing demands of the profession it is essential that teachers are better equipped, not less as Gove had us believe. It is right that teachers are experts in their specialist subject but also that they have thorough and continuing training in pedagogy, behaviour management and inclusion. Teaching is at the same time one of the most difficult and rewarding of professions and deserves acknowledgement and support.

Peter Downes, a County Councillor in Cambridgeshire, Vice-President of the Liberal Democrat Education Association, a former comprehensive school headteacher and a former president of the Secondary Heads Association, has expressed a forthright Liberal analysis of the Gove policy and has consistently set out the Liberal Democrat alternative.

Downes has written:

> "The fallout from the Academies Act will probably prove to be Gove's main memorial. He will be remembered as the man who personally undid a century of co-ordinated local democratic provision of state-funded education. We do not yet know whether the possibility of for-profit providers, possibly from abroad, entering the education market will materialise, but Gove has not ruled it out.

> [Gove's] pattern of intervention is riddled with internal inconsistencies and contradictions. Gove is reforming the national curriculum and at the same time encouraging schools to academy status so that they do not need to adopt it.

> While professing to want to make teaching a high status profession, he has removed the requirement for a professional qualification for teachers in academies and free schools, and

while claiming to want to make teachers more autonomous, he is specifying in greater detail than ever before what must be taught and at what age.

From Finland [Gove] takes the idea of teaching as a high status profession but ignores the fact that all schools in Finland are fully comprehensive, they don't start formal teaching until the age of seven and there is no national testing before the age of sixteen."[7]

Conclusion

At the time of writing, Michael Gove's successor, Nicky Morgan, has shown signs of being more sensitive to teachers' needs and to the role of local authorities, even though she has made no formal commitment to change. Time will tell. Education provision and policy is fundamental to the inculcation of Liberal values. It is important for Leeds, with its remarkable history of educational innovation and of exemplary high values, to avoid falling by default into the abyss of Gove's plausible but malign reforms. Liberal Democrats have got to have confidence in their beliefs and to have the arguments at hand to defend them under whatever tendentious and superficial arguments are proffered by the Conservatives. The Liberal case is powerful and persuasive; alas, it tends to be lost by default.

References

1. Wintour, Patrick, *Labour vows to rub out Michael Gove's education reforms*, [Online], The Guardian, 30 April 2014
2. Jenkins, Simon, *Schools are held hostage by politicians' control-freakery*, [Online], The Guardian, 2 May 2014
3. Jackson, Patrick, *Education Act Forster*, Madison, 1997
4. *Obituary of James Graham*, The Times, 16 September 1931
5. Who's Who, *Sir Alec Clegg*, A & C Black, London, 1986
6. Vaughan, Mark, *Summerhill and A S Neill*, OUP, 2006
7. Downes, Peter, *Bottom of the class for Gove*, Liberator 305, September 2012

– 4 –

TRANSPORT

Transport in Leeds

by Cllr Ryk Downes

In this chapter I will give my thoughts on where we are now with transport in Leeds. It is important to note that this is a constantly changing scene – there is always red tape delaying projects and nothing in transport ever seems to progress at the desired pace.

Combined Authority

The West Yorkshire Combined Authority came into being on 1 April 2014. Its membership comprises the five local authorities in West Yorkshire – Bradford, Calderdale, Kirklees, Leeds and Wakefield – and York, represented by the six council leaders and opposition politicians from these authorities and the chair of the Leeds City Region Enterprise Partnership.[1] There is an Overview and Scrutiny Committee of other councillors from the six authorities. The combined authority is responsible for a £1 billion West Yorkshire Plus Transport Fund. It has a strategic overview of transport projects for West Yorkshire and York. Through the Leeds City Region Enterprise Partnership it will work with private enterprise in promoting the regional economy. This is to be supported, as an integrated approach to transport is required across the region.

This new West Yorkshire Combined Authority has absorbed the previous West Yorkshire Integrated Transport Authority – known as Metro – and "Metro" is now the combined authority's brand for public transport.[2]

Whilst localism is important, certain aspects of transport are better dealt with holistically, specifically bus, rail and road networks. The benefit of this strategic body is that it should allow for devolved powers from Westminster for funding and approval process of projects. Far too often those in the south make decisions affecting Leeds when they are not in a position to witness first-hand the challenges of providing a modern day transport system for Leeds and the City Region.

Transport fund

When I was chairman of Metro I proposed a West Yorkshire Transport Fund whereby if all districts raised their precepts to pay into the fund the resulting money could be used to borrow, prudentially, £1bn for transport projects. At the time this was rejected. However, it is now back on the agenda and on 7 July 2014 the Prime Minister and the Deputy Prime Minister announced £420 million for a West Yorkshire Plus Transport Fund.[3] This should be supported and encouraged as a way of locally raising funds to help recover from decades of government underfunding of transport in West Yorkshire and York. It is sad to think though that this fund could have been up and running already and delivering on local projects. Another example of how transport has not been at the top of the local agenda for some time.

Nationally, figures show that of the metropolitan areas of England, Yorkshire and Humber in 2007-08 received the lowest funding per head and even today receives far less per head (£251) from government than London (£644). London with just 15% of the population of England received 34% of transport spending in 2011-12.[4]

Buses

At present buses are run privately for profit by operators. Where a bus service is not commercially viable it is subsidised by local councils. This system allows great freedom by the bus operators over where they run, what they charge and when they run, almost without external control. They can register a route anywhere and run it, altering it without consultation. Concern in the past has been about when services are cut in frequency or removed altogether, leaving people without the service they rely on. If a service is cut completely the local authority can put it out to tender for an operator to run it with subsidy; but these services are usually only hourly at best.

In recent years too, bus operators have used the increasing cost of fuel as an excuse to increase fares, when fuel amounts to only around 14% of their costs. So a ten pence a litre rise in diesel amounts to around 1% on their cost. When fuel prices have, on rare occasions, come down the operators do not rush to drop their price. It is interesting to note that major bus operators hedge their buying of diesel which means that price fluctuations do not affect them for many months. So in theory a more stable pricing regime should be possible.

It is my view that the inexorable increase in price, coupled with buses missing and reduced frequencies and routes has led to the decline in the patronage of buses. In many cases almost to a core of people that have no other option than to use the bus. I would advocate cheaper prices to compete with other modes. Short bus journeys are very expensive in comparison – the bus industry has to an extent priced itself out of the market. More should be done to attract young people and leisure users onto buses. A bus ticket could provide so much more than paying for a journey. It could be linked to offers at cinemas, restaurants, leisure attractions. This would also help relieve parking pressures at such places.

A much better system would be to move to Quality Bus Contracts which would allow the authority to set the routes, fares, etc. This would provide a fixed income for operators, whilst keeping control within the authority. It would also give tighter control over monitoring the services and ensure they run to time, or don't fail to run and when the first and last buses run, otherwise the operators would be penalised.

Trying to use a bus in Leeds at the moment can be confusing. You can ask for a day return ticket and be sold an operator's ticket which will only work on that company's buses or, for a premium, a Metro dayrover can be purchased which allows transport on all buses. What is by far and away a better system would be a smart card; this would allow a passenger to travel where they wished to on which ever company's bus without penalty or having to look which bus it is to see if it is valid. This should also be extended to incorporate the rail network. The technology already exists to do this and in fact the software has been purchased already by the local transport authority. It should be put in place as a matter of urgency.

When the Liberal Democrats were in coalition in Leeds a FreeCityBus was introduced to connect the train station to the Town Hall, LGI (Leeds General Infirmary), University, Civic Hall, the Headrow and Leeds Bus Station. Under the current Labour administration this was made into a paying service with a flat fee of 50p. This service should be re-instated as a free service and also made to run up to St. James's Hospital, thus connecting the city's two hospitals.

Park and Ride
There are very few park and ride schemes in Leeds. There should be more, providing free parking and regular ten minute bus services into Leeds from the outer ring road or nearby district centres. This would help to relieve congestion on the arterial approach roads to Leeds. Many commuters drive into the centre to park their cars, often in makeshift car parks; the park and ride schemes should be cheaper than the car parks to encourage commuters to park way before they get into Leeds. The park and ride buses should be express services, only picking up at the park and ride on the way in and only dropping off at the park and ride on the way out of the city centre to give a fast journey so it becomes a quicker and cheaper commuting option.

Trolleybus
Successive governments have blocked trams coming to Leeds, leaving Leeds as the largest city in western Europe without a rapid transport system. Trolleybuses deliver everything that trams do with regard

to getting people out of their cars and onto public transport into the city. However, if Leeds is to be the only British city with trolleybuses it would leave it vulnerable to increased maintenance and purchase costs due to lack of buying power.

There is growing resistance to the current proposals due to local residents' concerns. Bodington Hall, a university hall of residence, was originally the terminus of the route through Headingley, but this has now closed. The route is proposed to go further to Holt Park, but concerns over adequate parking and environmental impact remain, for many, unresolved.

Trolleybus is seen by some as a poor alternative to the failed supertram bid. Whilst it delivers most of the benefits, a high quality ride, mass transit and quicker journey times and would get people out of their cars, many still see trolleybuses as they used to be prior to them being shelved in the 1960s. Trolleybuses have moved on a lot since then. If we are to have them, an eye should always be kept on the possibility of converting the network to trams at some point in the future.

Electric buses

A watching brief should be kept on this emerging technology as this would be a good environmental option, but at present there is not the proven technology or range for them to be considered in Leeds. The other drawback with electric buses is that they do not attract car users from their cars. To do so requires a permanence of route. A bus route can change easily, a tram or trolleybus cannot. This appeals to regular commuters, who can rely on the service when making the decision whether or not to use public transport.

Bus/train interchange

Leeds bus station is about half a mile from Leeds train station. In an ideal world for public transport the bus station would be moved to Sovereign Street to provide an interchange between the two. At the moment, for anyone wanting to go from the train station to the bus station there is no clear route. It can be done, but is not clearly signposted; this needs to change.

Trams

Trams would currently be the best option for Leeds, for urban and inter-urban connectivity. A tram system can be built up over time by borrowing against future ticket revenue. Initial lines have already been identified to Holt Park and to Stourton from the city centre. A loop around the city is also required. Further routes would be to Seacroft, Elland Road/Morley, and could link up with a proposed tram/train network, which then could expand over time to the whole City Region to improve connectivity. The benefit of a tram system is that it carries a high volume of passengers per vehicle and with the infrastructure gives a permanent feel to the route. Also the quality of ride is generally superior to that of buses.

Trains

At present trains to Leeds station are run under a franchise system with the government. The local transport authority is a co-signatory only to the Northern franchise, which means that locally there is little control in developing the specification of this franchise, nor in the running of it. The Northern and TransPennine Express franchises, which cover most of the north of England, are up for renewal shortly.

Control of these franchises should be devolved to the area they cover. This would mean setting up a rail board in the north made up of councillors representing the areas concerned, as they are in the best position to know what is required. When the Northern rail franchise was awarded it was done so with zero growth (meaning that the operator did not have to grow passenger numbers, or provide for any such growth); this was a big mistake. Rail usage in Leeds has grown in recent years to a point where trains have become overcrowded and a victim of their own success. There has not been enough investment in rolling stock due to the nature of the franchise and it has fallen to local authorities to work with local agencies and rail companies to buy stock. Some of this money has had to come from increased ticket prices.

Leeds has a good link to London, but journey times, whilst reasonable, need improving. High speed rail would help achieve this whilst maintaining the existing traditional network and freeing up capacity for freight, especially through to the Humber docks. This in turn would take some of the freight off the motorways relieving congestion and improving journey times to Leeds.

The coalition government has announced a new station will be built at Kirstall Forge. More stations should be built, for example Horsforth Woodside, Thorpe Park, East Leeds Parkway, Armley, Elland Road, Calverley, Parish Church, White Rose, Holbeck, Methley, Ardsley Park and Ride, Osmondthorpe and Arthington.

On the whole rail fares are more competitively priced than buses, but need to be integrated with either parking fees or bus fares to make them more attractive, so that passengers only pay once, ideally through a smart card, for their entire journey.

TransPennine Express
This is an important line for connections from Hull to Liverpool; however the service needs improving as it is often at capacity. There are currently four trains per hour from Leeds to Manchester, four per hour from Leeds to York, but only one per hour from Leeds to Hull, and likewise one per hour from Leeds to Liverpool. These figures need to be higher: six per hour from Leeds to Manchester and half hourly services from Leeds to both Hull and Liverpool.

Harrogate Line
This is an old diesel line and is in desperate need of electrification. More importantly though this line could be altered to provide a tram/train service (see below) which could also connect Leeds Bradford Airport, which has no direct link to Leeds. A spur could be taken from

the existing Harrogate line just south of the Bramhope tunnel; but for heavy rail this would be difficult due to the gradient involved unless a very expensive underground station were built at the airport terminal. Light rail can cope with the gradient and so a through line could be built which connects through to the Wharfedale/Airedale line going through Guiseley and Apperley Bridge to Bradford.

Wharfedale/Airedale line

Whilst this line has been electrified, and provides a good service for commuters, in the rush hour trains are often standing room only. However the nearest station to Leeds is Guiseley, so the standing time, whilst not desirable, is not too long.

Tram-Train

This mode of transport is long overdue in this country and what better place to introduce it than Leeds? With the railway station being full to capacity this would offer the opportunity of bringing commuters into Leeds by rail, but without overcrowding the station. At present the government is conducting trials in South Yorkshire, but the technology is long proven in Europe and the trials should easily have provided the information necessary to run them in England.

The first route to benefit from Tram-Train should be the Harrogate line: this would allow for more stops on this well used line, but also a more frequent service, as tram-trains can run on line of sight stopping rather that electronic signalling. They could branch off the main rail line around Burley Road and go into Leeds via Wellington Street, thus terminating outside the Train Station and freeing up much needed capacity for additional services.

HS2

Whilst a great idea in principle (the desire to connect Leeds to London with a much quicker service), concern has to be raised over the route which must be sorted out. Initially the proposal was to go to Manchester first and then to Leeds after, this would be disastrous to Leeds and its economy. Thankfully the argument for a 'Y' shape network has been won and assuming Manchester does get HS2 Leeds must not be left out or all the investment will be seen to the west of the Pennines. HS2 will also free up capacity on the classic network and allow for move local services and the possibility of bring more freight back to the rail network.

Underground
Whilst this is aspirational and would solve many transport issues and remove many public transport users from the highway network, the cost would be so prohibitive as to make it unviable. Estimates are that it would cost £220m a kilometre. The underground terrain of Leeds is not easy and whilst an engineering solution could be found at this moment in time it would not be realistic to fund such a scheme.

Cycling
The topography of Leeds makes cycling challenging for those who are not fit. Recent changes to allow hackney carriages into bus lanes should be reversed; many cyclists expressed concerns over these proposals as they feel more vulnerable. If they are to remain, the potential to expand the system to allow private hire into these lanes as well should be avoided. More segregated cycleways are required and better facilities for parking bikes. However there should also be a safety campaign as many cyclists choose not to have lights on their bikes and flout traffic laws, to the frustration of other road users.

Cars
Cars cause congestion and pollution, and an awareness campaign should be launched once a rapid transport system is in place to encourage as many commuters out of their cars and onto public transport as possible. One way of doing this would be to build more park and ride facilities, as mentioned earlier. For cars coming into Leeds, whether to park and shop or to get from one side of Leeds to the other, the road system is not easy to navigate. With the Arena being located to the north of the city, this will only get worse for those

accessing via the M1 and M62. Clearer signage is needed to ensure that cars which do not need to cross the city centre do not do so. For car parking a clearer plan should be put in place which from outside of the centre directs people to numbered car parks and indicates them from the inner ring road.

Air

Leeds is home of Leeds Bradford Airport, located in Yeadon. Whilst a fast growing international airport with destinations throughout Europe, North Africa, Pakistan and New York, it suffers from a lack of connectivity. It is more than half an hour from the nearest motorway (M62) and has no fixed link to Leeds. These should be near the top of any priority list.

There are two options for a rail link. In the short term a rail halt could be built just south of the Bramhope tunnel and the station could be served via the airport's own car park shuttle bus system which already goes nearly half the distance from the terminal to the long stay car park. Access would be via a new service road and ideally a fifteen minute service should be offered. The benefit of this would be that as passengers fly into Leeds they can be taken directly from the terminal to the nearest rail line, without having to go though much traffic. At present you would have to go Guiseley or Horsforth and to do so would mean a longer journey that could get one held up in traffic. This does not have the feel of a train link to the airport whereas an airport halt would. The second option, a longer term solution, would be to take a tram-train off the Harrogate line at the same point, as discussed already.

Conclusion

Leeds needs cheaper buses that are more regular and offer more value. They need to be brought under local control via Quality Bus Contracts. We also need a rapid transport system that can expand over the City Region. Existing train lines must all be wholly electrified and future franchises designed, awarded and monitored in the areas they serve.

A fixed link to the airport is required and a new faster access road to the airport needs building.

Whilst I have advocated the immediate use of smartcards, Leeds should continue to look for new and innovative solutions to ticketing. The increased use of the internet, smartphones etc. for cashless transactions needs to be explored and implemented as soon as possible to put Leeds at the front of the technology queue for a change. But caution should also be exercised so as not to exclude traditional payment methods for passengers who are not able to embrace modern technology.

Bibliography
1. West Yorkshire Combined Authority, *First meeting for Combined Authority*, [News release], 28 March 2014
2. METRO, *Metro becomes part of West Yorkshire Combined Authority*, [News release], 31 March 2014
3. Leeds City Region Enterprise Partnership, *Billion Pound Deal for Leeds City Region*, [News release], July 2014
4. HM Treasury, *Public Expenditure Statistical Analyses – October 2012*, [Online], 2012

CULTURE

Youth culture

by Vitus Asaga Bawa

When asked to write a piece about culture my initial response was no problem, I mean every one knows what that is, right? Well talking about it is another thing completely. As I discovered when I first sat down to actually tackle what is fundamentally one of the most important, yet understated concepts of the human experience.

What I needed was a definition, something that summed up what it was and in my research I came across two that stood out:
1. that which is regarded as excellent in the arts and manners.
2. the term developed to refer first to the betterment or refinement of the individual, especially through education, and then to the fulfilment of national aspirations or ideals.

From that I built my own, making the third one:
3. the popular ways and methods in which a society aims to exist, better itself and reach for its future starting with the individual.

According to Robert L. Peters "Design creates culture. Culture shapes values. Values determine the future".

The origin of art is traced back to "the cave man times" which is damn near the beginning of our existence, ergo it would be fair to say art is an innate part of the human experience, which over the years we have refined and redefined until we got to where we are today.

The digital age

Interesting fact: today, there's more calculating power in a pocket calculator than we used to get to the moon.

As that sinks in I'd like to point out the obvious fact that the number crunching machines of yesteryear have made their way into every orifice of today's civilised world, and that's not changing any time soon, without the advent of some truly horrific cataclysmic event (and let's leave Kim Jong-un out of this). The only change will be the speed at which it grows – and that is only going to get faster.

A question I'd like to ask here is simple....why? There are many reasons. Let's take it from an artistic stand point:
– Less/ no loss of quality of work
– Easier to edit and change
– No need to restart
– Easier to share

Before I get ahead I'd just like to outline the fact that without education, none of this would be possible. In my opinion the last big jump came with the then modern sciences and influences of the Moors, who are widely accredited for laying the foundation for the rennaisance.

The Moors, the Renaissance and da Vinci

I don't think you can informatively discus this period without at least a mention of this man – Leonardo da Vinci. He has often been described as the archetype of the Renaissance Man, an Italian Renaissance polymath (avid learner) he was in his time a: painter, sculptor, architect, musician, mathematician, engineer, inventor, anatomist, geologist, cartographer, botanist, and writer. His genius, perhaps more than that of any other figure, supposedly, epitomised the Renaissance humanist ideal (culture if you remember). He, like many others in his age, could not have expressed his mind had it not been for the influences of the Moors - the medieval Muslim inhabitants of Morocco, western Algeria, Western Sahara, Mauritania, the Iberian

Peninsula, Septimania, Sicily and Malta. Their territory compromised much of what is now Spain and Portugal, and a part of France. There was also a Moorish presence in present-day southern Italy after they occupied Mazara until their last settlement of Lucera was destroyed in 1300. Not much is thought about them but in fact they are widely accredited by many historians for a lot of the intellectual engines we use to sustain and develop our civilisation today.

Take for example the concept zero. According to Nick Snelling in his article "What did the Moors do for us":

> "The Moors in Spain were also famous as astronomers and mathematicians. Indeed, algebra comes from the Arabic al-jabr and the previously unknown, and critically important, Eastern concept of zero (probably originating from Babylonia) was introduced to Europe via Spain".

That doesn't have too much to do with art and culture until you consider this: without them moving us on from roman numerals, modern engineering, the sister to design and the then modern techniques of spacing and lighting in Leonardo's art would have been very different. Also binary code, "the language of computers", which at its root is comprised of vast quantities of ones and zeros, would not exist.

And one last thing before we move on: the muse

I have adapted the meaning from Arabic dictionaries as: a poetess who is inspiring, often seen as a goddess or woman (modern equivalent is a star). According to a documentary I watched about the Moors, they (muses) were pretty much very intelligent prostitutes who could entertain their customers, so basically stars in today's terms. They were accredited with being the pioneers of the modern concept of rhyming. Without them I personally would not have been able to produce the work I did for my campaign on indiegogo. (I mentioned the Leeds Yellow Book on there – www.indigogo.com)

hi my name is V, I'm the man times 5
so I'm often referred to as we
if you speak Japanese you can call me bui
and that's no translation
it's the true relation, it's real
like my passion put in practice
no hesitation
you can only name it skill
cuz self meditation
got me on a path of true elevation
now I'm here for the people
who love the thrill
no segregation
I have an idea to make it open for those of you who will
and are loving the arts
got my business head on
still speak from the heart

I need that access, so this is my stage
I'm playing my part
please check out my proposal after this song is played.
or go back to the start
and basically help us get played and payed, my team stuck
behind me
cuz so far a path's been paved
now I wanna make a motorway
please let us live today
and let the future say
eyeee
those guys embodied the great
or better, you're dealing with the verbal professor
could you be a treasured investor
is that a maybe or yes sir?
or a quick onomatopoeia, wham bam and
thank you mam

caress the feeling of love
repping the peace like the dove
Lyrics provided by Mor.v.us

So that brings us nicely back to the 21st century.

Role models
Currently the people in the media eye can be said on average to be promoting a lot of negative, non productive nor educational stuff. Leeds needs to take a stand in providing more morally wholesome role models and giving more attention to positive movements. A good way to do so is for the entertainment industry to reflect as a whole what we feel. It seems like we are in the middle of morally trying times, which I believe are not totally unlinked to our financial turmoil. No doubt we are all working harder than ever before, well most of us anyway, but in my opinion, our proliferated culture of selfishness and greed (you know the high and low profile people I'm talking about) is one I don't wish to put mine and my readers' consciousness through.

Where are we going?
Currently, nowhere, not fast and if we are its backwards. Honestly compared with the progression of the tools and resources we have, what we're doing is negligible in terms of innovation, research and development (there is no need for it).

I'd now like to take the time to point a "two middle finger salute in the direction of the recession". My own example shows the general problem, Personally, and without too much reference to the pain caused by what is a semi-necessary, fully avoidable and wrongful tightening of the country's purse strings, I'll say this: Due to the "hatchet harry" style cuts, I have been personally affected by the new set of rules in the following ways:

Education
I had to drop out of Plymouth university course of robotics because

even though I was tested by faculty staff and declared a sufferer of dyspraxia (difficulty with numbers) I wasn't allowed any help so therefore I fell further and further behind on the numerical tasks till it was pointless to carry on, given everybody else's level of progress. I was given the option of restarting the year with the same costs and restricted grades, but I decided employment suited me better at that time and I dropped out.

Housing

I was informed that I could get housing benefit with my then other half after we moved in together. Upon doing so, I tried to claim and I discovered this as a non-truth. I was on a course of self employment so jobs which were hard to come by were even harder to attain. This meant my eighteen year old ex was left to tackle the issue of rent pretty much by herself...after six months of this our once happy home and relationship fell apart.

Employment

I'd like to say I am by no means "work shy". For example, a) I haven't even discussed funding for writing this piece, I hope you can feel my mind, heart and soul has been placed in it, and b) since sixteen (I'm now twenty-two) or shortly after I have had no less than eight jobs, at least half of which have been fully commission-based, the last of which was a great office job and which was not commission-based. After living on roughly £33 a week or less for four months prior and during this period, and finally finding a house an hour and a half's walk away from my new place of employment, I was hardly in a condition emotionally and financially to turn up to work, fully fed, motivated, with clean clothes and a healthy attitude. I did not make it past the probation period. My mistake, I'd say, was taking on as many shifts as I could because I knew I needed it. By the way, I was successfully taxed £35 out of the £170 I made from that period.

After signing back on, at the first or second meeting I had with my advisor, he was doubtful that I'd been trying hard enough to find work.

I was "sanctioned" for a month and a half and, except for the cheque from the last job, I received nothing. I find it harder to believe than you do. I do not wish to publicly discuss how I've survived so long. One of my biggest worries is whether my phone will ring these days with a job opportunity, I'm worse off than the last time and I cannot even express what this does to my self esteem. I rarely leave my bedsit. There are many young people in exactly the same sort of situation.

Where we should be going

Leeds is a leading city, quite simply we are third in the UK for business and are renowned for shopping, but we need to be making more use of our aforementioned heritage status – we have a lot of it tucked away. For example the Cottage Road Cinema is the oldest cinema in Leeds and one of the oldest cinemas in the UK in that it has been continuously showing films since 1912. This was in a year in which roller coasters where just coming into fashion. (I mean cinema only came of age in the 60's according to Billy Liar in the Big Issue) I had no idea of its existence, despite it being only a 20 minute walk away from me. The future is digital – we all believe so and we now need to focus on the interactive.

How to make ends meet

We need to take the initiative by backing companies who will lead us into the digital age. We need to invest more in renewable energy and biodegradable products. We should create more jobs by sponsoring the making of interactive tour systems, using the new technologies I've mentioned and selling these systems once they've been updated.

Breaking the illusion that there isn't enough to go around is important, because there is. From my standpoint, the problem is that we are just managing it poorly and not distinguishing well enough between those who find it hard to work and the ones who think it's better not to.

And with this we should see more life in the Leeds culture. I finish with one of my poems:

The Path to Farewell
by Vitus Asaga Bawa
So where did we leave it off?
We know we are lost
Amongst the insults like gunshots And do it now at all costs
I feel like I'm parking without a spot.
Ricochet. So that rectangle leaves your vision tangled on the dot
For a moment on the clock, one 28th of a second
As time heals all
Can it mend those pieces of Gods broken heart ?
He doesn't allow evil deeds, no you did That time you bared witness to it

Yet did nothing for it to stop
I've watched it on my few short stints as the victim
Never gave survivors guilt a chance ,
It took my boy in nursery school under my command
It moved that pick up "We're missing our ride!"
We grabbed onto its back as it pumped into a stride
He was panicking more than I
I shall not tell you what I did with the last of my strength
As he sat and watched me from that corner
With the last of my few conscious moments
We both knew for what was happening there'd be no recompense
Now just me hanging on as he was safe
Not a scratch not a cut, not a dent.
From this moment dear Lord you prevent me from having to repent
I should end it here But this is a sonnet not a limerick
I fear
Which is which I care not know
I'm getting past the ebb, now on with the flow
If you asked me smoking doesn't kill as much as its cause

All y'all know Now all you chesty coughers hold your
applause
I see you nod Cuz the truth I saw may set you free
Agree, its intrinsic I'll show no remorse for what I. believed
I had to do
And this was a relief as much for me as it was for you

Now should I say mushi-mushi Or weave with adieu.

Thank you.

– 6 –

HEALTH

Social media and public health in Leeds

by Dr Anthony Lockett

L eeds is a city with about 750,000 inhabitants and as such is the third largest city in the UK. Its wealth and prosperity are based on financial and commercial services and it is the largest centre for financial legal and business services outside of London. Leeds is considered a Gamma World City – a city that brings regional economies onto the global stage according to the Gamma World City 2010 study. This places Leeds alongside Phoenix, St Petersburg and Valencia.[1]

A quarter of the working population of Leeds is employed in financial services – a sector that is heavily reliant on the internet. As a result Leeds has a well developed internet infrastructure; it has been awarded the title of "Wi-fi capital" by News Corporation. Public use of wi-fi is twice the national average in Leeds, making it one of the most connected cities in the UK.[2]

Public health in Leeds
The health of the inhabitants of Leeds is generally worse than the England average. Deprivation is higher than the national average and over 30,000 children live in poverty. The life expectancy for men is 12.4 years lower for men and 8.2 years for women in the most deprived areas compared to the least deprived areas of the city. The incidence of heart disease stroke and cancer is higher than the national average, and estimated levels of unhealthy eating, smoking and obesity are higher than the national average.[3]

In April 2013, Leeds City Council took over the public health functions of the defunct primary care trust – abolished as a part of the NHS reforms. The functions transferred included the statutory programmes of
- Sexual health services
- NHS health check programme (for those aged 40-74)
- Health promotion
- Public health advice
- National Child Measurement Programme

and the discretionary public health functions of
- Obesity
- Physical activity
- Substance misuse (drugs and alcohol)
- Stop smoking services and interventions
- Children 5-19 public health programmes
- Nutrition initiatives
- Health at work
- Programmes to prevent accidents
- Public mental health
- General prevention activities
- Community safety, violence prevention and social exclusion
- Dental public health
- Fluoridation

The council has identified tackling inequalities, smoking cessation and child health as priorities for the £40 million it receives from the Department of Health.[4]

Health and the internet

Since the inception of the internet, the medium has been used to make available medical information. The ease by which information can be passed on the internet has led to claims that it can provide major health benefits. However, as until recently websites and other internet connections were static, the benefits have been limited. This situation changed with the advent of social media.

What is social media?

Social media is defined as, "A group of internet-based applications that build on the ideological and technological foundations of Web 2.0 and allow for the creation and exchange of user generated content".[5] The foundation of social media, Web 2.0, refers to the creation of dynamic websites compared to static homepages used in the past. So, while the general principles of the internet remain intact, there are several differences with Web 2.0 as it permits billions of users to be online, and these users can edit, generate and comment on content published online. This advance has been permitted by the next generation of web browsers, that permit advanced searches and browsing on the internet and offer advanced editing features as standard.

One of the principal advantages of social media is that it does not require any specialist IT knowledge. Starting a new blog or posting a video can be done in a few seconds.

Social media and healthcare

The advent of social media has opened new channels of information for patients and healthcare professionals. "Medicine 2.0" is generally used to indicate the use of social media among healthcare professionals, while "Health 2.0" is associated with the use of web tools to improve healthcare. All stakeholders in healthcare can benefit from the use of social media; studies have shown that social media can be an efficient tool to disseminate information and improve patient care.[6]

The use of social medicine in healthcare has, however, significant limitations. Privacy and legal issues arise when doctors share medical cases online or give medical advice. Despite these limitations, social media is changing the way we acquire and share information about healthcare and healthcare professionals.

Healthcare professionals are now in a position to prescribe information for patients in an evidence-based manner. This so-called "information therapy" could improve patient outcomes, but it is recognised that the availability of online information does not necessarily improve decisions made by patients and professionals alike. However, it is accepted that prescribed information can improve patients' satisfaction and compliance. While the value of prescribed information is accepted in the management of individual patients, can prescribed information be of wider value in the management of public health, and particular the social determinants of public health?

The determinants of public health

In Leeds and other major cities people living in the most deprived areas can have life expectancies up to 12 years less than those in more affluent areas. These differences can be attributed to "social determinants of health".[7] The social determinants of health include: social organisation and stress; unemployment and the labour market; social support and cohesion; food and nutrition; poverty and social exclusion; life course.

Social organisation and stress

Research has shown that it is plausible that psychosocial environmental factors like the organisation of work; social isolation and a sense of control over life can affect the likelihood of developing and dying from chronic diseases such as diabetes and cardiovascular disease. Stresses caused by the psychosocial environment provoke biological responses in humans that are damaging to health. The impact of social organisation on health is mediated by three main factors: material circumstances, psychological factors and health-related behaviour. These act in conjunction with early life experiences, cultural and genetic factors to promote disease. The final mediators of diseases related to stress appears to be the neuroendocrine system which reacts to stress by causing a range of biochemical and metabolic changes that promotes disease.[8]

Unemployment and the labour market

There is a well established link between unemployment and health, but the nature of the link is not clear. People with ill heath are more likely to lose their jobs and find it harder to gain employment. So there is a selection effect in the employment and health relationship, as well as the effects of stress in terms of health-related behaviour. The effects of unemployment are not the only impact of employment on health. Labour market flexibility is also a determinant of health. Labour market flexibility, while it has reduced the unemployment rates in the UK and USA, has led to the creation of large numbers of low paid jobs that are often associated with high levels of job insecurity. Research has shown that these low paid and insecure jobs can be as stressful as being unemployed. Indeed there is some evidence that whereas the stress of unemployment appears to plateau, the stress of job insecurity is prolonged. Job flexibility may therefore be a contributor to poor health. A particular link has been established between coronary heart disease and psychosocial work factors.[9]

Social support and cohesion

There is considerable evidence that social isolation leads to ill health, yet the reason behind the relationship is not clear. Social support – resources provided by other persons – is important as it leads an individual to believe that they are valued and belong to a society. The strength of social support can therefore be measured in terms of the number and frequency of contacts. These measures do not reflect the quality of the contact, however. Support can be also measured by its content. The content of support can be emotional, practical or informational. Emotional support includes self-appraisal and esteem, practical support includes practical and financial assistance, while informational support includes information to assist a person in health care and behavioural decisions. In the provision of social support the source of the support is also important. Emotional support has a different meaning depending on the source and close relationship support can have both a negative and a positive impact. Social support involves interactions between people. Providing support has a reciprocal nature and can affect the health of the supporter. Social support has been shown to have a great impact on mortality, for example the role of marriage in reducing mortality amongst men.

Social support works at a society and an individual level. Evidence suggests that societies with a high degree of cohesion have better health than those with low levels of social cohesion, in terms of mortality and morbidity.[10]

Food and nutrition

Policy makers have an increasing understanding that major gains in public health can be made by implementing social interventions in food and nutrition. In Europe nutrition is a substantial contributor to the burden of disease, through cardiovascular disease and diabetes as a result of salt intake. Interventions to reduce obesity and hypertension have had dramatic effects in public health. Measures designed to overcome food inequality – food shortage due to poverty – can also have an effect on population health in poor populations.[11]

Poverty and social exclusion

Poverty – or the degree of deprivation – and social exclusion in a society has a major impact on health. Quite often both of these factors are found in minority populations, and hence the burden of ill health can be greater in these populations. Poverty and social exclusion affects health in a number of ways. Poor and excluded populations often have difficulty in accessing health care, live in poor housing in areas with pollution and have limited ability to have the resources to adopt health improving behaviour.

Life course

The life course is the combination of biological and social elements that interact with each other to produce health. It brings public health into a course of a person's lifetime. Health can therefore be said to be the sum of the accumulated advantages and disadvantages of health status imposed by social circumstances. Such accumulations tend to cluster both in groups of individuals and over time. For example, research shows a person living in poor housing is more likely to have a hazardous job and being educated means that a person is more likely to have an occupational pension.[12] The life course causes ill health in a number of ways. First there is a direct relationship; poverty reduces the access to health care interventions. For example poverty leads to diet restriction, poor diet leads to folic acid deficiency, leading to a clustering of neural-tube defects in the lower social classes. However, in some cases the links are indirect and difficult to identify – for example the links between birth weight and social status. A prime factor in life course accumulation is social mobility. Life course accumulation tends to constrain social mobility, as those who are not socially mobile tend to get left behind.[13]

Can social media improve public health?

There are concerns that health benefits accrue to those with social media access, who may not need these benefits due to their social status, while there is some evidence that projects which blur the digital divide can result in information benefits for those who cannot normally access social media. If the digital divide can be broken down what are the potential benefits that could be found? The evidence is as follows, taking the social determinants of public health in turn.[14]

Social organisation and stress

The effect of internet-based public health interventions on diseases caused by social causes – such as smoking and diabetes has been variable. For example, fewer than 20% of type two diabetics with internet access enrolled in a diabetes management programme. Those least likely to respond were ethnic minorities and male – where the burden of disease is most prevalent. By contrast, the effects of web-based smoking cessation programmes were better. Thirty per cent of those randomised to an internet smoking-cessation program quit compared with 12% in the control group. The reason for the differences appeared to be the support offered.

Unemployment and labour market structure

There is evidence that access to social media can counteract the health problems induced by unemployment and job insecurity. Unemployed people with social media access appear to have a better sense of wellbeing and self-efficacy (which is a measure of the belief that an individual can achieve their goals and aims). However, the evidence is that social media can mitigate labour market related ill health only in certain circumstances. The higher a person's educational achievement, the greater is the benefit. So it is unlikely that general increase in public health could be achieved by increasing access to social media. In contrast, for those in employment an increasing number of companies are offering wellness programmes that are internet delivered. These programmes have been successful in some areas such as smoking cessation.

Social support and cohesion

There is considerable evidence that social media is a good facilitator of social support. The possibility for anonymity, asynchronous communication exists and, freed from the limitations of time and space, emotional, practical and informational support can be delivered by the internet and have an effect on health. The magnitude of the benefits is hard to quantify, as there is a lack of robust measurements. It is evident that social media can improve self-efficacy, while at the same time improving adaptive coping – changing behaviour to avoid health risks.

Food and nutrition

Weight loss and nutrition is one of the most common health intervention delivered over the internet. Several randomised clinical trials have shown web-based weight loss interventions to be effective for short-term weight loss. It has been found that an internet behaviour therapy group is more effective than internet education in promoting six month weight loss. A 2003 follow up study extended these results, showing that the addition of email counselling to the internet behaviour change group increased the amount of weight lost.

However, the evidence suggests that the magnitude of weight losses in internet weight loss trials is less than that found for individual or group treatment approaches. Greater weight losses are typically observed for internet weight loss interventions that are highly structured, provide support from a human counsellor, utilise tailored materials, and promote a high frequency of website logins. These programmes typically produce weight loss over a six month period – unlike conventional programmes.

Poverty and social exclusion
There is no evidence that the internet improves the health of the poorest elements of society. Indeed it is possible that digital divide may actually increase social exclusion, by empowering the already empowered.

Life course
The life course is a concept that exists at the interface between biological and social factors. Without an influence on both it is not possible to say if an intervention can influence the life course. In certain circumstances such as weight loss the life course may be altered, but in other public health circumstances – such as cohesion and poverty – the life course is not likely to be changed.

Barriers
The review of the effectiveness of social media and internet-based interventions on public health has highlighted the barriers to widespread health gains from these interventions. They are: implementation, reach, scalability and costs, maintaining interest, compliance and utilisation, the need for tailored messages.[15]

Implementation
One of the obvious benefits of using social media to improve public health is the creation and maintenance of virtual communities. However, public health interventions often do not use social media, due to the complexities of implementing social media projects on a large scale. The potential for wider scale health benefits may be not achievable until combined interventions that influence the life-course are developed for Web 2.0. The exception is public health emergencies, such as outbreaks of influenza where the widespread dissemination of information has the potential to assist in preventing the spread of infection.

Reach
Reach refers to "the absolute number, proportion, and representativeness of individuals who are willing to participate in a given initiative, intervention, or program". As many interventions are frequently focused on a single outcome (e.g. smoking cessation or dietary change) and, as a consequence, may appeal to a relatively small niche portion of the overall population with internet access, the issue of reach can be major. The few population trials of internet interventions have shown generally low reach rates, despite their use of high-quality internet interventions. For example, Glasgow et al[16] found that only 2%–5% of overweight adult members of three large managed care organisations participated in a free internet weight loss program. Perhaps most challenging was that key population segments – those over age 60, smokers, those estimated to have higher medical expenses, and males – were less likely to enrol. Reach is also a potential issue for ethnic minorities, where internet use is lower.

Scalability and costs
Scaling an intervention for delivery to a large population is not a trivial endeavour and understanding the scaling process is essential to the success of an intervention. Most internet research interventions are hosted on shared servers, a low-cost, easily administered solution that is appropriate for the low volume of traffic often encountered in research studies. However, at scale, different architectures (e.g. multiple servers, application servers, search databases, session databases, and redundant storage systems) are necessary. An inverse association is likely to exist between population size and the marginal costs of intervention implementation. Consequently, internet-based interventions may be too costly for some populations (e.g. rural practices, community health centres). Therefore, cost considerations will remain primary drivers of adoption.

Maintaining interest
Dropout rates in the 40%–50% range are not uncommon in internet-based interventions. The evidence is that many participants simply

lose interest over time particularly if interventions are of low intensity and are not highly structured.

Compliance and utilisation

Website utilisation is one of the more consistent predictors of positive outcomes. However, website utilisation tends to drop rather precipitously after the initial weeks of intervention participation. Unfortunately, we know little about those factors (at the individual or group levels) that are associated with sustained website utilisation. In the absence of such data, a number of strategies have been employed with some success. For example, reminders and follow-ups and promotional offers have limited success in improving utilisation and compliance.

The need for tailored messages

Emerging evidence supports the use of tailored messages in internet interventions. Briefly, the tailoring process combines large repositories of health messages with data about individual participants to provide highly personalised health messages to individuals. Tailoring can be performed on any number of individual characteristics (e.g. age, gender, location, self-efficacy, readiness) and has been shown to outperform traditional, static health information strategies across a wide range of outcomes. An important area of future research is to determine how, and under what circumstances, tailored messaging might be used most effectively to stimulate sustained website utilisation.

Although most investigators accept that tailored approaches are preferable, few trials have systematically determined the type or extent of tailoring necessary by outcome. Tailoring complexity has a strong relation with the associated costs (at least during development) and given the wide range of variables that can be used to tailor messages, guidance about best practices is needed.

Using social media to improve the health of Leeds

Some of the public health problems in Leeds might be amenable to social media intervention. Smoking and weight loss in particular are problems that could be tackled. Leeds with its IT infrastructure appears to be well placed to implement social media-based changes, but there are some barriers that need to be overcome.

While the less deprived areas of Leeds have internet speeds of up to 10Mb, the most deprived areas have much slower speeds, at the same cost as the more wealthy areas. This is not due to the differences in suppliers; the same internet service providers cover all of Leeds. The reasons behind the differences in Leeds are liable to be infrastructural, and are possibly due to the availability of fibre optic and other cabling that permits more rapid data transfer. The differences are large. For example in LS6 speeds of up to 10Mb are available, while in the most deprived parts of LS7 and LS8 – including areas such as Shepherds Lane – speeds are generally 4-5Mb.[17] This restriction will limit the interaction elements of social media and its content and reduce reach. It will also have an impact on scalability and therefore cost, as the cost of infrastructural changes would be prohibitive. There must be no delay in implementing the Leeds City Region's West Yorkshire Local Broadband Plan to ensure all areas have access to superfast broadband by 2015.

Leeds City Council in its role as provider of public health services should provide public health interventions in some of the most deprived areas in England to overcome the digital divide in Leeds. This entails:

- Working with web designers that can develop solutions and interventions across a wide range of platforms – including smartphones, tablets and PCs.
- Developing tailored solutions for the people of Leeds. In the deprived areas educational attainment can be compromised – children in the deprived areas attain less than the national average in GCSE, while in year six 19% are obese.
- Working with NHS practitioners to publicise the services, and to ensure co-ordination.

- Identifying individuals that have fallen through the safety net – by allowing interaction and the collection of data of individuals that have not agreed to enrol in a programme.

Of all of these proposals, the use of the internet to identify individuals at risk of the disease is perhaps the most controversial as it introduces mass screening for disease at a local level. Screening programmes are controversial as they are costly and time consuming. For a screening programme to be acceptable and successful, they need to be directed towards an important health problem for which there is a diagnosis and accepted treatment, while the disease is early or latent. These restrictions have, by and large, limited screening to national programmes that might or might not benefit local health.[18] The use of social media permits the use of the techniques of screening at a more local level. This will allow a better targeting of resources for screening, but there are two counterpoints. If local mass screening is to work, access to healthcare interventions must be improved generally.

Second, there is the perception that the use of social media in this context is intrusive and that forms of consent are needed. In reality the concerns about privacy and screening are general to all forms of screening and relate to the ability of an individual to control their own destiny. This is the concept of autonomy. Autonomy in the classical sense is related to restrictions imposed on individuals to improve health. The use of social media gives a new dimension to autonomy – the use of autonomy to promote health.

Leeds is ideally placed to make the most of the changes the NHS reforms have permitted. Its role in public health services permits it to directly intervene in supporting public health. Previously with the existence of the Primary Care Trusts, the implementation of public health initiatives was fragmented. The proposals would have other benefits. The creation of a multi-platform social media solution would facilitate the peer-to-peer communication across healthcare providers, and permit the rapid dissemination of information.

Conclusions

Reports on the benefits of internet interventions for public health issues have been encouraging. However, the successful interventions may only benefit limited populations in special circumstances. Therefore however, much remains to be done.

1. Align public health priorities with internet and social media developments

While the success or failure of interventions is regularly documented, how they fit into the needs of the population that the interventions are seldom addressed. This will involve the development of new metrics that better capture utilisation as well as attrition.

2. The development of Web 2.0 platforms

The better development of Web 2.0 tools will permit wider involvement of citizens in public health issues. It should not be expected that clinicians and the public should keep pace with Web 2.0 developments. Instead, policy markers should more actively engage with web developers to develop population-based interventions.

3. Develop new outcome measures

The traditional outcome measures of life expectancy and quality of life may not capture the benefits of internet and social media public health interventions. Outcome measures that reflect the sustainability and reach of interventions are needed to better quantify the benefits. This is also the case for measures of autonomy of the public.

Some of the public health problems in Leeds can be addressed using the internet and social media. Leeds has already in place an extensive wi-fi network. However, for Leeds to capitalise on the benefit of the internet in public health in addition to the above challenges, ways must be found to bridge the digital divide. In the case of Leeds, this has less to do with access but more to do with download speeds. Finally, and perhaps most controversially, targeted life style and other interventions are needed for individuals and populations.

Without these issues being addressed, it is unlikely that breaking down the digital divide will be sufficient to reap significant benefits form internet and social media based interventions in public health in Leeds.

The desire to implement changes and initiatives across the whole NHS, and the naïve failure to appreciate the necessity and benefits of the "postcode lottery" – better defined as "local innovation" – has severely delayed and inhibited innovation in public health interventions. Recent efforts to introduce IT initiatives across the NHS have been expensively disastrous. The proposals in this paper will gain traction by being demonstrated effectively as a Leeds initiative.

Endpiece

The proposals contained in this document are not new. However, similar approaches have previously been performed by commercial companies and social media intervention services and solutions are available commercially already, but the focus is on individual health – either by subscription services or employers purchasing packages for employees. There is no example of population-based interventions, for the simple reason that it is difficult to see a commercial profit from such a venture. It is precisely for that reason that these proposals sit within the Liberal agenda and would assist the generation of a fairer society. Through these developments, the Gamma City of Leeds should be able to harness its potential to intervene in public health issues using the internet.

Bibliography

1. Wikipedia, *Global City*, [Online], 2013, http://en.wikipedia.org/wiki/Global_city
2. Wikipedia, *Leeds*, [Online], 2013, http://en.wikipedia.org/wiki/Leeds
3. Public Health England, *Health Profile 2013 - Leeds,* Crown, 2013
4. Leeds City Council, *Council to take Public Health lead*, [Online], 2013, www.leeds.gov.uk/news/Pages/Council-to-take-public-health-lead.aspx

5. Kaplan, Andreas & Haenlein, Michael, *Users of the world, unite! The challenges and opportunities of Social media.* Business Horizons, 53 (1), pp59-68, 2010

6. Van De Belt, Tom, *Definition of Health 2.0 and medicine 2.0; A Systematic Review,* Journal of Medical Internet Research, 12 (2),e18, 2010

7. Marmot, Michael, *Status Syndrome,* Bloomsbury, 2004

8. Brunner, Eric, *Stress and the Biology of Inequality,* BMJ, 314, pp1472-1476, 1997

9. Marmot, op. cit.

10. Brunner, op. cit.

11. Van De Belt, op. cit.

12. Bartley, Mel, Blane, David & Montgomery, Scott, *Health and Life-course: Why Safety Nets Matter,* BMJ, 314, pp1475-1478, 1997

13. ibid.

14. Bennett, Gary & Glasgow, Russell, *The Delivery of Public Health Interventions via the Internet: Actualizing Their Potential,* Annual Review of Public Health, 30, pp273-92, 2009

15. ibid.

16. ibid.

17. cable.co.uk, *Compare broadband, 2013,* [Online], www.cable.co.uk/compare/broadband

18. Juth, Niklas & Munthe, Christian, *The ethics of screening in healthcare and medicine,* Springer, 2012

ECONOMY

The economy of Leeds and the Leeds City Region

by Ian MacFadyen

Ending poverty in all its forms as quickly as possible is the aim of Liberal Democrats. Liberal Democrats in the coalition, in Leeds and the Leeds City Region and across the United Kingdom are building a stronger economy in a fairer society, enabling every person to get on in life. Providing the workless with work on at least a living wage and ensuring fair distribution of the fruits of the economy of Leeds and the Leeds City Region is the way to end poverty. All citizens in Leeds must benefit according to their needs, regardless of age, gender, ethnicity, faith, disability or ability, social class, sexual orientation, or background. Councils can help create the conditions for job creation by the private and third sectors and can work with central government, the private sector, the third sector and others to ensure fair pay and fair distribution of the wealth Leeds produces.

Deputy Prime Minister Nick Clegg and the Leeds City Region Local Enterprise Partnership – comprising Barnsley, Bradford, Calderdale, Craven, Harrogate, Kirklees, Leeds, Selby, Wakefield and York – have negotiated the City Deal,[1] a plan for a stronger economy in the City Region with new powers which sit alongside the councils' new General Power of Competence in the Localism Act 2011.

Scanning the economy

As noted in an earlier chapter, Leeds is the third largest local authority by population[2] in the United Kingdom and larger than two member states of the European Union, Luxembourg and Malta. With 2,952,057 people,[3] Leeds City Region Local Enterprise Partnership is the largest outside London, with a larger population than Northern Ireland and six European Union member states. The value of the Leeds economy in 2011 expressed as Gross Value Added (GVA) was £18 billion, the fourth highest after London, Birmingham and Greater Manchester South (Manchester, Salford, Stockport, Tameside and Trafford) and just marginally higher than Glasgow. GVA grew fast in Leeds up to 2006, but between 2006 and 2011 it was 5%, lower than Greater Britain as a whole, Birmingham, Glasgow, Manchester and other northern cities, except Hull.[4] GVA across the Leeds City Region was £54 billion, 4% of the total for the United Kingdom.[5]

People in Leeds work hard and their output shows the strength of the Leeds economy and how much more can be done. The GVA per employee in 2011 was £43,000, the highest in Yorkshire and higher than Birmingham and most other comparable areas except Edinburgh, Glasgow and Greater Manchester South, but lower than Great Britain as a whole.[6]

Output across the Leeds City Region, as shown by GVA per employee, was £17,700 in 2010, higher than in Yorkshire and the Humber as a whole, but lower than the average of the United Kingdom. GVA per person in the Leeds City Region was much higher in 1997. There do not appear to be any reasons for the reduction since then that could not also apply to other regions.[7] The sectors that contributed positively to GVA – production, construction, distribution, finance and insurance, business services, public services, property[8,9] – are expected to reverse the shrinkage of the last ten years and grow by between 17% and 47% over the next ten years, so that the whole Leeds economy grows by 30%. The Leeds City Region Local Enterprise partnership's plan is to increase GVA by 2.6% a year to 2030.[10]

The business of business
In 2011, 24,700 businesses were active in Leeds, slightly fewer than

the year before but significantly more than five years earlier. Leeds is second to Birmingham, which has a fifth more businesses, and Leeds has a quarter more businesses than Glasgow, which is next after Leeds. Since 2006 Leeds has had higher growth in the number of businesses than the averages for Great Britain and the Leeds City Region, but in six cities – Aberdeen, Glasgow, Edinburgh, Manchester, Bristol and Newcastle – the growth in the number of active businesses was higher. Forty three percent of businesses in Leeds and the Leeds City Region survive for at least five years, the sixth highest rate of business survival in Great Britain.

Businesses in Leeds and the north of the City Region say their business confidence is improving. Confidence is growing most in the service sector and there is some improvement in manufacturing confidence. Nearly two-thirds of businesses in the service sector and manufacturing report higher turnover than when the recession began in 2008, but most service companies and manufacturing companies are operating below capacity. Over half of manufacturing respondents say they are under pressure to increase their prices because of the costs of their raw materials.

Homes, gardens and parks not dereliction

Large derelict sites with surface parking make Leeds and other parts of the City Region look blitz-scarred and show that Leeds and parts of the City Region did not recover from recessions before the current recession began during the Labour government. Dreary eyesores like parts of Quarry Hill testify to market and political failure, which can drive away the entrepreneurs needed to move the economy forward and create jobs. Instead, to make the city better for the people who live here and attractive to investors and job creators, derelict sites should be made available to local authorities and housing associations to build affordable homes, or be turned into temporary public gardens and urban parks, as Liberal Democrats announced when the party led the administration in the city council and as was done at Wellington Place, where development has now begun. The council's General

Power of Competence provides the legislative means, if there is no other. Legislation is needed to enable local authorities to tax derelict land and land kept undeveloped in land banks.

P60 and UB40

Some 504,000 people are of working age in Leeds and are self-employed, employed, or unemployed.[11] There were, in 2013, 62,000 self-employees in Leeds and this number is expected to grow by 11% in the next ten years. There were 457,000 employed people in Leeds – fewer than half of these are women. There are expected to be 11% more people in employment by 2023, with the growth in female employment higher than for men. This increase in total employment will be slightly higher than the expected growth in Leeds's working population. The total number of people in employment in the Leeds City Region in 2013 was 2,473,000 and this is expected to grow by 8% by 2023.

In 2013 23,297 people in Leeds were unemployed and claiming Job Seeker's Allowance. That was 4.6% of those of working age. Across the Leeds City Region, the figure was 4.3%, about the same as for the United Kingdom as a whole.[12] Twice as many men as women were unemployed and a third of unemployed people have been unemployed for more than a year. There were 6,310 unemployed people aged 16-24, 13% fewer than in 2012, 3,470 were aged 50 and over, about the same as in 2012. Adding claimants of Invalidity Benefit/Employment Support Allowance and Lone Parent payments, the total number of people in Leeds who were unemployed and claiming out of work benefits in February 2013 was 64,510, or nearly 13% of those of working age.[13]

Cold numbers do not convey the emptiness of being unemployed, the slow corrosion of dignity with each passing day and the growing sense of the pointlessness of applying for work that deepens with each unsuccessful application. Each day the chance to gain skills and experience or use existing skills and experience becomes more remote before disappearing. Fortnightly attendances at the Job Centre Plus are fixed points in otherwise empty diaries that are almost looked forward to. All the time, there is the wait and anxiety about whether benefit payments will come and whether they will pay the rent or the mortgage, pay for the electricity, gas, water, telephone and council tax, food, shoes and clothes, and dinner money for children. The children's eyes dim to a flat despair the longer unemployment goes on and you worry night and day about them and when, if ever, you can provide them with the life you intended. Will they also have a life on the dole? If there are no children, will the money keep a roof over your own head, food on the table and clothes on your back?

Work can give dignity. Work can give self-government, the ability to provide for yourself and your family and the confidence to participate fully in civil society.

Unemployment is a scourge. It is highest in Gipton and Harehills ward – 12½% – and Burmantofts and Richmond Hill ward – 11%. No other wards have unemployment rates in double figures, but Armley, Beston and Holbeck, Killingbeck and Seacroft, and Middleton Park wards have unemployment rates of over 8%.[14] A fifth of households in Leeds have no one in them working. This figure was a little lower five years ago and is slightly higher than for the United Kingdom as a whole, but, while it is significantly worse elsewhere,[15] it is a disgrace that politicians should waste no effort in remedying.

The Leeds City Region's economic plan is to create 60,000 jobs to return unemployment to restore pre-recession employment levels,[16] but unemployment levels in 2008 were not acceptable and population growth means that just to stand still more new jobs are needed than have been lost.

The City Region and the Department of Work and Pensions should identify workless households and with the private and third sectors provide targeted programmes of training, including career changing retraining, and supported entry or re-entry into work. The City Deal's "Guarantee to Young People" offers 20,000 opportunities of "access to a job, training apprenticeship, volunteering or work experience", through a 14-24 Academy with a business-led curriculum, an apprentice training agency, apprenticeship brokerage for young people and employers, and a City Region alternative to the national contract for 16 and 17 year olds.

In addition, action by the City Region Local Enterprise Partnership will create between 4,500 and 7,400 jobs by 2018.[17] This is hardly enough. Something similar is needed for families and middle-aged and older people seeking work following redundancy, or forced to work into later life to complete pension entitlements or simply to make ends meet.

Nearly half of businesses in Leeds and the north of the Leeds City Region, had tried to recruit staff during the second quarter of 2013, more than in the previous quarter, but most had difficulty in finding suitably qualified staff. Two-thirds of service sectors companies and three quarters of manufacturing companies responding said they were operating below full capacity.[18] The City Region has assessed that productivity in the region is significantly below the average for the United Kingdom.[19] This suggests that job creation could lag behind any increases in production and demand as the City Region's economy improves.

More people will have to become self-employed and create their own businesses. With imagination, a way should be found to turn benefits into start-up grants, with safeguards to maintain entitlements if businesses fail. These grants should be for unemployed individuals who want to start out on their own and groups of unemployed people wanting to start co-operatives and social enterprises.

Rebuilding the economy

The City Council's vision is for Leeds to be the best city in the United Kingdom by 2030. The Leeds Growth Strategy focuses on seven sectors: health and medical; financial and business services; low carbon manufacturing; creative, cultural and digital; retail housing and construction; social enterprise and the third sector.[20] Agriculture is not included, but to help the sector, the City Council recently decided not to apply the Community Infrastructure Levy to farm buildings.[21]

The City Region Enterprise Partnership has made agreements with central government on business-friendly planning and a low carbon economy. Besides youth employment (already mentioned), the City Deal provides a £1 billion transport fund (see Ryk Downes' chapter on Transport) financed by a levy on councils in the new West Yorkshire Combined Authority and a promise of funding from the Department for Transport in the next Parliament[22] (which could be changed by the government of the day). The City Deal also provides an investment fund of £200 million from pooling business rates and other local resources, and a trade and investment strategy.

The draft trade and investment strategy[23] aims to increase substantially inward investment and increase exports in order to change the City Region balance of trade deficit of over £1 billion a year into a surplus of £600 million by 2015. Both are optimistic aspirations, given past regional and national performance. The Chamber of Commerce has found latent interest in exporting among its members.[24] The strategy includes reshoring or onshoring, which is the emerging trend of bringing manufacturing back to the United Kingdom. Leeds-based Premier Farnell has moved production of its credit card-sized computer from China, but to Wales, not Leeds.[25]

The Local Enterprise Partnership and central government have established the Aire Valley Leeds Enterprise Zone in East Leeds,[26] but full development may be delayed by reported difficulties in finding operators for one of the sites.[27] Unfortunately, Leeds was unsuccessful in its bid to be the location of the new Green Investment Bank (which went to Edinburgh) because Leeds's ability to recruit and retain relevant staff was judged to be weak.[28]

In the strategy, investment would be attracted for five "investment hubs", which are "based on concentrations of expertise and industry", not specific locations, and cover the sectors mentioned earlier in this chapter: health innovation, advanced digital technologies, decarbonised energy generation and biorenewables, financial services intelligence, and powertrain and precision engineering. Food and drink may be added as a sixth hub.

Construction, tourism, and transport and supply chains are surprising omissions, considering the housing and infrastructure needs of the region, its attractions to visitors and its strategic location at the confluence of routes within the United Kingdom and to the continent and beyond. Agriculture and forestry are also omitted, despite the City Region – and Leeds itself – being largely rural and the Local Enterprise Partnership suggesting in 2011 that it was an advocate for rural areas.[29]

On 7 July 2014, The Prime Minister and Deputy Prime Minister announced a £1 billion Growth Deal with the Leeds City Region Enterprise Partnership. This covers housing, development, business growth, an energy hub and skills development, as set out in the City Region's Strategic Economic Plan, and a new West Yorkshire Plus Transport Fund. Making the announcement, Deputy Prime Minister and Liberal Democrat Leader Nick Clegg said:

> "The Leeds City Region Growth Deal will create thousands of jobs, provide incredible new training opportunities for people, improve transport connections within West Yorkshire and to other cities across the north, allow new homes to be built, support fast growing businesses and build a stronger economy and a fairer society."[30]

The other 38 Local Enterprise Partnerships also received Growth Deals, but the Leeds City Region's Growth Deal is the largest over the allocation period. The Leeds City Region Enterprise Partnership is also preparing for central government a European Union Structural and Investment Funds Strategy in order to take oversight of strategies for European Structural Fund spending, which is also being devolved by the Coalition.

When and who

Planning is good. It will release money and powers from central government, setting Leeds and the City Region freer for some burgeoning of local innovation. Good planning can help ensure the long-delayed recovery takes place and that unemployed people can find suitable jobs with decent pay. It can transform Leeds and the City Region into the city and region of opportunity. But, too much planning can delay action and lose sight of the urgent necessity of meeting people's needs for work and opportunity without delay.

People need to see as well as feel that standards of living are improving. So, there should be an annual independent public and published audit of the Leeds and Leeds City Region economy. Among other things, it should examine the number and quality of jobs being created and taken by unemployed people in the Leeds City Region and whether recruitment is fair and without bias.

Responsibility for ensuring that plans are put into effect is diffuse within Leeds City Council, between the City Council and the City Region and between them and the forthcoming West Yorkshire Combined Authority, and, despite devolution and the promise of more, between the city, the City Region and more than one central government department. Diffusion can frustrate action. There needs to be someone responsible for the city and regional economy and for carrying out all these plans, accountable to the people of Leeds and the City Region through their elected city and district councils. Ideally this would be the same person for Leeds and the whole Leeds City Region; otherwise there could be more diffusion and disagreement. The need is for, in effect, a Leeds and the City Region minister for the economy.

Endpiece

This chapter describes the economy of Leeds and the Leeds City Region and the need for the two to work in hand to improve opportunities for people throughout the City Region.

The chapter recommends that: to make Leeds and the City Region better to live in and more attractive for investment and job creation, derelict sites should be turned into temporary public gardens and urban parks; jobless households should be identified and given targeted programmes of training and supported re-entry into work; similar help to that planned under the City Deal to young people should be offered middle-aged and older people; benefits should be turned into start-up grants for unemployed people wanting to become self-employed and start their own businesses; construction, tourism, transport and supply chains, agriculture and forestry should be included in the City Region's Trade and Investment Strategy; there should be an annual public audit of the Leeds and Leeds City Region economy; there should be a Leeds and the Leeds City Region minister for the economy accountable to the people through city and district councils.

References

1. Cabinet Office, *Unlocking growth in cities: city deals – wave 1*, London 2012
2. Office for National Statistics/Leeds City Council, *Leeds - The Big Picture: A summary of the results of the 2011 Census*, [Online], 2012
3. Office for National Statistics, *2011 Census: Usual resident population by local authority*, [Online], 2012
4. Leeds City Council, *The Leeds Economy (Monthly Economic Briefing) August/September 2013*, Leeds, 2013
5. Leeds City Council, *Leeds City Region – Latest GVA Data: Briefing note, February 2013*, Leeds, 2013
6. *Leeds Economy (Monthly Economic Briefing)* op cit
7. Leeds City Council, *Leeds City Region – Latest GVA Data*. op. cit.
8. ibid.

9. *Leeds Economy (Monthly Economic Briefing)* op.cit.

10. Leeds City Region, *Our economic plan Leeds City Region,* Leeds, 2013

11. ONS, *Leeds-The Big Picture,* op. cit.

12. Office for National Statistics, *Statistical Bulletin: Labour Market Statistics August 2013,* [Online], 2013

13. *Leeds Economy (Monthly Economic Briefing)* op cit

14. ibid.

15. Office for National Statistics, *Workless Households for Regions across the UK, 2012,* Newport, [News Release], 2013

16. *LCC Our economic plan* op.cit.

17. Cabinet Office, *Unlocking growth in cities* op.cit.

18. Leeds, York and North Yorkshire Chamber of Commerce, *Quarterly Economic Survey Q2 2013,* Leeds, 2013

19. Leeds City Region, *Quotation for key sectors policy for Leeds City Region: Project brief,* Leeds, 2013

20. Leeds City Council, *Economic Strategies,* Leeds, 2013

21. National Farmers Union, *NFU welcomes infrastructure levy u-turn,* York, 2013

22. HM Treasury, *Government prioritises long-term investment in infrastructure spending - Chief Secretary to the Treasury outlines the government's infrastructure investment priorities beyond 2015,* London, [News story], 2013

23. Leeds City Region, *Leeds City region Trade & Investment Strategy Consultation Draft,* Leeds, 2013

24. Leeds, York and North Yorkshire Chamber of Commerce, *Beyond Borders Realigning the Leeds City Region Economy Towards Export-Driven Growth,* Leeds, 2013

25. Supply Management, *News Focus Bringing it all back home,* Stamford September 2013

26. Leeds City Region Enterprise Partnership, *Aire Valley Leeds Enterprise Zone,* Leeds, 2011-13

27. *Timing Setback for Enterprise Zone ambitions,* Yorkshire Evening Post, 2 October 2013

28. Department for Business, Innovation and Skills, *Location of the Green*

Investment Bank: outcome of review of possible locations, London, 2012

29. Leeds City Region, Hinton S, LCR Strategy Manager, presentation, *The Leeds City Region Progress so far,* Leeds, 2011

30. Leeds City Region, *Billion Pound Deal for Leeds City Region,* [Online], 7 July 2014

– 8 –

COMMUNITY

The vital need for community

by Michael Meadowcroft

The strengths of free peoples reside in the local community. Without local institutions a nation may give itself free government but it has not got the spirit of liberty.[1]

The first of May 2008 was a more significant date in the development of community in Leeds than most people realised. It marked the first election for the Alwoodley Parish Council after a successful two year local campaign for the establishment of a statutory parish. Leeds already had 31 parish and town councils but the key difference is that Alwoodley is the first parish council to be established that is entirely within the old Leeds County Borough

It was no coincidence that Alwoodley – which was itself a late inclusion within Leeds in 1925 – should be the pioneer, being the richest neighbourhood in the old county borough and having the benefit of a significant Jewish community which played a key role in the campaign, but it gives hope for other "townships" in Leeds potentially to go down the same track. Having a parish council, with the power to levy a small supplementary rate, is by no means the only mark of a community but it does provide the framework to avoid some of the problems and tensions that can bedevil community associations. I shall return to this local theme but, first, we need to look at the background to the concept of community and to determine what Liberal attitudes and policies should be.

Probably no word in politics is as misused as "community." Time and again it has become a talisman on the Right for the replacement of a public service, and on the Left for the politicisation of voluntarism. It is such a sufficiently vague term as to permit every user to define it anew as suits the moment. It is time to recapture the concept of community as a vital component of human society and to develop policies which will restore it to its key role in the stability and integrity of the political process in its broadest sense.

There is an urgent need for action to revive and restore the sense of "belonging" which has been subtly eroded over decades. When Elizabeth and I moved to Bramley in 1981 the lady who sold us the house held a "house cooling party" for all the neighbours that had been part of her life over the years. We were also invited and at one fell swoop we met the electrician, the plumber, the decorator and the joiner etc. Today, only one of those neighbours is left and, despite sporadic efforts at communication we hardly know any of their replacements. Equally, I used to note when returning to Yorkshire from London how virtually everyone passed the time of day in the street. Now, I deliberately try to catch the eye of passers-by as they pass my bus stop but hardly anyone has a "how d'you do" nowadays.

The word "community" is used legitimately in a variety of contexts. We talk about a "community of interest" to denote a group of people without any necessity for a specific location, who share a common enthusiasm for a cultural activity, opera, say, or chamber music, or for local history. We use the phrase "international community" to describe the United Nations, or the European Union, or key diplomats who co-ordinate their help for a particular country of region. Even when approaching the substance of our modern definition of it as a geographic community broadly recognised by its inhabitants as an identifiable entity to which they instinctively "belong", there are those who have always struggled to promote community organisations which exist across a number of neighbourhoods, united, for instance, by being focussed on council tenants.

Definition

For the purpose of this chapter, and its emphasis on the need for strong, vibrant, diverse and interdependent communities (to underpin the application of wider policies, including housing, planning, social services and the arts) I have to essay a definition. This book is concerned with Leeds and is mainly concerned with urban society. In any case, "community" in rural areas is largely a village and will usually have – or can inaugurate – a statutory parish council. In my urban context, I regard a community as being a geographic neighbourhood, generally identified, or capable of being identified, as a "township." Such communities are largely self-defining and of varying size depending on history and geography. This is inevitably and essentially vague but clear lines on the map are only required if and when a community wishes to become a statutory parish, otherwise there is no harm in having a debate over what names belong to which communities. In any case planning developments over decades have often eroded the spaces between previously separate communities. I have taken to putting "Bramley" regularly into my address to make the point that I live in a township which has always had its own identity but which is increasingly regarded as "West Leeds" and just a suburb of the city. This assimilation by the big city is continuing beyond Bramley and other "out townships" of Leeds.

Before the local government reorganisation of 1974 the borough of Pudsey was a freestanding municipality situated between Bradford and Leeds. The government had to make an arbitrary decision as to which city it should be included in and chose Leeds. Now I have begun to see Pudsey described as "West Leeds" in the local press. Curiously, after local government reorganisation, Pudsey ended up without a town council, unlike Morley, the only other municipal borough within Leeds, which formed a town council and which continues to fight its corner for its community.

There are manifestly different "communities". We refer, for instance, to the "international community" and there are religious communities and communities defined by their ethnicity. In the political sense, however, and within the compass of this chapter, I define "community" as a geographic entity, with self-defined boundaries, whose membership comprises all those who live within those boundaries, whether they participate in its communal activities or not.

Development

Communities develop by evolution rather revolution. The splurge of new towns, particularly following the war, transplanted significant numbers of people into new houses on swathes of vacant land, with only the small nucleus of an existing village alongside. They had no pre-existing collective identity and usually very few older people. Those who took these houses often complained about the anonymity of the towns and it has taken a number of generations for them to develop a greater sense of community. Historically, politicians, with the best of intentions, have believed that they were benefiting their community by transforming its physical environment – demolishing slums, building high rise flats, planning clinical but impersonal estates – rather than the less visible, more sensitive and increasingly complex task of achieving an enhanced sense of belonging to a neighbourhood and greater opportunities for community participation.

Throughout my time as an elected representative, both on the City Council and in Parliament, I was regularly told that the problem with politicians was "too much talk and too little action." I have always disagreed. In politics, and particularly, in post-war politics, there was far too much action and nowhere near enough talk. All too often the politicians have wanted to have some physical memorial to their period in office rather than the rather amorphous but more Liberal aim of implementing policies which enhance linkages and underpin human values.

Historically, housing conditions in parts of Leeds were so appalling that housing reformers, such as the socialist Rev. Charles Jenkinson, saw their mission being to demolish the slums of Hunslet and Holbeck and to replace the dwellings with hygienic modern houses and flats.

Such was his determination that when Labour came into office in 1933 Jenkinson's plan to demolish 30,000 slum dwellings and to replace them with the equivalent number of new homes within six years became council policy. Only just short of half of these figures were achieved, not least because Labour lost control of the city council after only two years, (and Jenkinson lost his own seat a year later) but, in terms of houses, Leeds was transformed.

The problem was that the close knit communities of south Leeds could not simply be transplanted elsewhere and, indeed, only one new house could be built for four or five demolished on the original site. Consequently the community was dispersed and its longstanding linkages broken. Ironically, today some of the most difficult council estates in Leeds are those built by Jenkinson, including, for instance, parts of Gipton. There appears to have been little concept of the importance of the community and its strengths, but one cannot lay too much blame at the door of the reformers of the 1930s for being unaware of the deleterious effects of the break up of strong working class communities in the pursuit of better housing conditions.

Paradoxically the revolutionary project that is most associated with Charles Jenkinson is the one that, from a community point of view, worked best and yet was never really appreciated. Completed in 1938, Quarry Hill was a massive block of 938 dwellings in a huge oval, with a mixture of two, three, four and even five bedroom flats, with an innovative refuse disposal system and a wide range of planned community facilities, not all of which were built. Many of the tenants had moved into Quarry Hill together with their neighbours, and the common services made it possible to develop a real community spirit and made it a self-contained neighbourhood of some 4,000 people, very close to the city centre. By 1978 the flats needed substantial spending on its structure and it was estimated that £7 million was needed to give it another 30 years of life. Those living there wished to remain but only the Liberal group supported them. The other parties, not attuned to the concept of community, saw only the somewhat forbidding grey exterior rather than the lively community within the walls and they voted for demolition.[2]

The undermining of communities in Leeds continued with an obsession with the clearance of the old terraced houses. Both Labour and Conservative groups supported the policy, differing only on the speed of clearance. Whereas there was a case for the clearance of slums that were incapable of improvement, there seemed to be no awareness of the possibility of adding dormer windows and installing inside bathrooms and toilets in most old houses, with the consequent prize of keeping communities intact.

When Liberal councillors returned to the City Council from 1968 they promoted a policy of improvement not demolition with considerable support from residents who wanted to retain the links with their neighbours and their community. As a consequence many parts of Armley and Beeston, which were then represented by Liberals, still have their back-to-back and through terrace houses. The added advantage of these houses, particularly as house prices continue to rise faster than inflation, is that their relatively lower prices give an opportunity to young couples to start out on the house ownership escalator.

Hard on the heels of the myopic adherence to the area demolition policy was a new passion for high rise development and for "walk up" maisonettes. Again, although there was no technical reason why residents in blocks of flats could not be involved in community activities, they tended to be psychologically cut off from life outside the confines of the block. It was not as if this had not been perceived well before the 1950s and 1960s; with commendable foresight, Alderman Frederick Lupton and his colleagues had written in 1906:

> The Committee consider that land is so easily attainable at a low price within a mile of the most crowded parts of the City, that it is quite needless to introduce flats... into Leeds. Whilst there are objections to them on the score of want of privacy, as

well as giving proper exercise to young children, who cannot come down from the upper storeys in high buildings, and are therefore shut up the dwellings whenever their mothers (sic) cannot look after them, The same objection applies when one considers the case of the old and infirm.[3]

Even worse for community identity were the "system built" flats with their much hyped – and as was soon seen, unachievable – slogan of "streets in the sky." Leeds had just one development, Hunslet Grange in Leek Street, which soon became known locally as Bleak Street. Built in 1968 with some 2,500 units it had continuing problems of dampness and its isolation made it unpopular, particularly with families. Liberal Councillor Denis Pedder was derided for predicting in the early 1970s that Hunslet Grange would be demolished in his lifetime. Even the expedient of using it as student accommodation failed and it was demolished in 1983. Denis Pedder lived for a further twenty years after this date!

Leeds communities

These City Council actions were not taken with malice aforethought, but they certainly militated against Leeds' communities thriving. Efforts by Liberal councillors to focus on the broader concept of community, rather than only on improvements to the physical fabric, were mis-represented by both other parties as being opposed to progress. However, despite all the pressures, the old communities refused to disappear and in neighbourhoods such as Armley, Bramley, Kirkstall, Beeston and New Wortley there were efforts to promote social meetings and local activities, such as local history research, locally published magazines and books. In the more affluent areas, such as Headingley and Oakwood, residents' associations flourished.

The huge problem, outside of the old communities that still retained an identity, was the soulless nature of the new areas with acres of council housing. On these "one class, one tenure" estates – one of them stretching from Gipton to Whinmoor with some 80,000 council tenants – solid and respectable Leeds citizens were lost in anonymity. The early estates were designed on a circular basis that, no doubt in contrast to the lack of privacy of the slums, over exaggerated it, thus giving potential burglars good cover.

Creating the conditions for a community to thrive in such areas is difficult but not impossible. It takes some expenditure, including a building in which to meet and to house activities, at least one full-time worker and a determination to stick it out for the long haul. It may also require some demolition and new build, such as took place at the northern end of the Wyther estate in Armley, thanks to the persistence of Liberal councillor, David Selby. This area, the "Houghleys", was appalling and for a time had been used by the council housing department as a place of last resort for "problem" families. A purpose built community centre on the estate had had to be demolished after only some twenty years of life. The worst housing was demolished and replaced by housing association dwellings and, thus, private tenants. Further small scale demotion enticed private developers and home owners. The area is not without its lingering anti-social behaviour but the resulting mix has transformed the locality

There is a third type of geographic community that is important to Leeds and that is the neighbourhoods that become home to immigrants to the city. There has been a Jewish presence in Leeds for over two hundred years, including a number of wealthy wool merchants originally from Germany, but its main component was the huge influx of poor refugees from the Russian Empire, mainly present day Lithuania, Byelorussia and Poland, following the assassination of the Czar in 1881. By 1891 out of almost 8,000 Jews in Leeds, 5,500 lived in a small area known as The Leylands, on the east side of Vicar Lane, north of Kirkgate Market, and stretching up North Street to Skinner Lane.[4] The community had its own shops and synagogues and initially spoke almost entirely Yiddish. Despite the poor conditions, (the area began to be cleared as "unfit" by the city council from 1907) the Jewish children were the best school attenders in the Leeds and had fewer absences through illness. There was great emphasis on learning English and on bettering themselves. Thus they consistently moved northwards up Chapeltown Road to the larger houses there and eventually the plusher suburbs of Moortown and Alwoodley. One Jewish biographer calculated that the community moved northwards at the rate of one mile every thirty years![5]

The evident success of the Leeds Jewish community and its remarkable contribution to Leeds' business, professional and cultural life, despite its difficult origins and the considerable prejudice against its "alien" background, gives me optimism for the future of Asian immigrant communities in Leeds. There are, for instance, great similarities in the differences in background, language, religion and also numbers of the Muslim community in Beeston, off Dewsbury Road. The political challenge for the politicians and the community leaders alike is to learn the lessons of integration with cultural diversity as achieved by the Jewish community over the past century.

Community politics

The Liberal Party nationally officially espoused "community politics" in 1970[6] and the Liberal Democrats have carried forward the policy. Insofar as "community politics" is supposed to epitomise the party's policy on community campaigning and, by extension, its attitude to communities, it is important to analyse its theory and practice.

There is no aspect of Liberal, and now Liberal Democrat, politics that is as susceptible to manipulation as community politics. Although those who promoted the resolution in 1970 had a clear view of its philosophy, its antecedents and its successors have not been as principled. The two main names quoted as "modern" Liberals in local government at the time were Cyril Carr in Liverpool and Wallace Lawler in Birmingham. Both were remarkable councillors who won seats against the odds in their two respective cities, but their electoral successes were a consequence of grasping political opportunities, accompanied by excellent party organisation, concentrated on a small number of wards. Also, having been elected, they both did huge amounts of personal casework. Their continued success, and its expansion to other wards, was based on their local image of serving their constituents well personally at a time when this wasn't the norm. They epitomised a Liberal attitude to politics and to local representation but they were not "community politicians" in the sense of showing their constituents how to handle the council bureaucracy successfully themselves. In fact, it was pretty much the opposite, in that they deliberately espoused an attitude of "come to me to get things done", accompanied by regular local newsletters reporting on very parochial local issues, which was probably necessary for word of mouth to build up their reputations and to ensure electoral successes at the time.

In Leeds, following our first successes in Armley in 1968 – after an absence of 25 years from the City Council – we followed a similar prescription and only stumbled on elements of "community politics" by accident. We believed that citizens deserved and were entitled to information on the council's plans for them and their community. Councillors were provided with the council's phased programme of slum clearance showing when areas of the city were programmed for demolition. Armley was affected by this programme with almost all its terraced housing scheduled for different dates. Motivated by the naïve belief that our constituents were entitled to know the future of their homes, we simply copied the phasing map on to a clear street map of the ward and sent copies to every house. We were immediately attacked by both other parties for divulging privileged information and for fomenting local opposition to the programme!

Our action did indeed lead to many well attended local meetings and a broadly-based campaign for "improvement not demolition", which had a string of local successes at local enquiries. Every time I drive through Armley and see the rows of popular terraced houses off Town Street and at Armley Lodge, I see today the success of that "community politics" mobilisation where the councillors were the political arm of the people rather than encouraging dependency.

This was very different to the strategy of hegemony practised by the Labour party when in power. They are very ready to support local voluntary groups in the hope of suborning them politically, but they are quickly dropped when they show signs of independence.[7]

Years ago there was tendency in the party to name me as one of the "gurus" of community politics. This was particularly perverse as I spent much of my time critiquing the policy and expressing doubts as to how it was being interpreted on the ground.[8] Our experience in Leeds did, of course, have relevance to the policy and we tried to empower the communities in the wards we represented but it was difficult to do this when they were too easily bought off by promises of grants from the City Council.

Over the forty plus years since the "dual approach" resolution of 1970 far too much of what passes for community politics is simply drumming up casework, planning surveys on simplistic issues, running trite campaigns and petitions and delivering thousands of "Focus" leaflets reporting all this. The question I have often had to ask in Leeds is "What is specifically Liberal about this leaflet?" when, frankly, it could have been produced by any party. I find it depressing that I am still making the same points about the need for a distinctive local Liberal Democrat identity.[9]

Unless the active presence of Liberal Democrat Councillors and MPs instils an awareness and an acceptance of Liberal values in a community the party and its candidates will always be battling to to appear more active and concerned than its opponents, with the burden of perpetual Focus leaflets weighing down even the most dedicated activists. Eventually, charges of "instant compassion" and "mindless activism" acquire a resonance and the "two horse race" appeal wanes.

Liberal Democrat policy

Liberal Democrats, as with all politicians, have to work within existing constraints both physical and financial. We cannot, for instance, wish the high rise flats away, however much they are inimical to community identity and participation. They can, however, have communal areas, taking over a ground floor flat if necessary, and be made secure with the presence of a concierge.

The provision of a community centre is crucial to the health of a neighbourhood. Without somewhere to meet and to debate local issues it is difficult to envisage effective participation. Such a building does not have to be grandiose but ideally it should be big enough to have activities for local youths and facilities to provide refreshments. Experience shows that a local centre needs at least one full time staff member.

Where there is already a recognised community or, in a Leeds terms, a "township", there should be encouragement to inaugurate a statutory parish or town council. The procedure involved in achieving this status is understandably rigorous but, given goodwill, is not too complicated and the benefits are considerable. Parish status provides a statutory electoral process so that "leaders" are elected, thus avoiding the advent of the local demagogue who sooner or later puts off wide participation in a voluntary organisation. It also enables basic funds to be raised via a small additional precept on the council tax.

I believe that it is vital for the community to have its local schools. The recent attempts to promote academies and free schools are inevitably damaging to the integrity of the community. Education is not just a matter of focussing on achieving examination success. It is much more than that and the connection between the school, its students and their local community is vital if we are to produce well-balanced young adults who are aware of the needs of the community and of their responsibilities towards meeting them. Also, by being within the local authority's provision of services, they can benefit from a holistic perception of what each child needs.

This view of education, and the importance of keeping bright students within their community, applies also to professionals who serve "difficult" communities. Increasingly those who are looked up to in such an area do not live in it and instead commute to it. Teachers, doctors, social workers, lawyers and politicians rarely live in the areas in which they work. Amongst professional people it is often only the local church minister who lives within his or her neighbourhood. Unless professionals share the life of their community their broader influence is diminished and, worse, the example given to bright students is that success means moving out rather than taking a lead locally.

Following the serious urban riots of 1981 Nick Harmon, himself a Brixton resident, went further in suggesting reasons for the troubles:

> One common aspect of the riot areas is that all have suffered for decades because politicians and their planning advisers have removed from them their natural community leaders. Local councils have used central government funds to buy up, often compulsorily, anyone with a financial stake in the community – home-owners, shopkeepers, landlords, small businessmen – to add their property to the council's land bank, pending comprehensive redevelopment. Such individuals are the first to be offered the money and favourable housing nominations to move out of the area, if only because they are the most independent and mobile citizens. The effect has been to break the economic and social ties which bind the community together, ties which also help to police it.[10]

It applies also to policing. Even the community constable commutes to his or her patch. It is only by living locally within the community and sharing its life that the community police officer can hope to gain the confidence of the local citizenry and build up vital local intelligence. There are no powers to force professionals to live in "downtown" areas but financial incentives should accompany moral pressure for them to be more effective by showing day-to-day solidarity with their clients and colleagues.

Conclusion

It is Liberals' firm belief that the malaise increasingly afflicting local democracy can best be tackled at the local level. Individual men and women, by active involvement in a vibrant local community, are more likely to see the potential in the wider political world than if they have no incentive to abandon the television. Despite Mrs Thatcher's infamous statement,[11] we believe that there is certainly such a thing as society and that people are interested in involving themselves in activities which are intellectually and socially enjoyable and worthwhile. Individualism has its importance but it has gone too far. It is high time that we took the challenge to revitalise our communities seriously and to begin to restore the Liberal values that characterise human society.

References

1. Derounian, James, *Another Country: Real Life Beyond Rose Cottage*, NCVO, 1993
2. Ravetz, Alison, *Model Estate*, Croon Helm, 1974
3. Lupton, Alderman F M - Chairman, *Unhealthy Areas Committee: Housing improvement, A summary of Ten Years Work in Leeds*, April 1906
4. Freedman, Murray, *Leeds Jewry - The First Hundred Years*, Jewish Historical Society of England (Leeds Branch), 1992
5. Raisman, Geoffrey, *The Undark Sky, A Story of Four Poor Brothers*, p 300, Harehills Press, 2002
6. Liberal Party, Resolution on a *"dual approach to politics, working both inside and outside the institutions of the political establishment"*; resolution adopted at the Liberal Party Assembly, Eastbourne, 1970
7. Meadowcroft, Michael, *Diversity in Danger*, pp50-53, Beecroft Publications, 2009
8. See also for instance *"Problems in Community Politics"*, notes for speech at ULS Conference, [Online], November 1972, www.bramley.demon.co.uk/liberal.html
9. Meadowcroft, Michael, *In My Heart and my Soul - Chapter "Standing Firm – Linking Campaigning to Values"* Association of Liberal

Democrat Councillors, [Online], August 2012, www.bramley.demon.co.uk/liberal.html

10. The Economist, 18 July 1981

11. Thatcher, Margaret, *"You know, there is no such thing as society. There are individual men and women, and there are families"*, Women's Own, Interview, 31 October 1987

APPENDIX 1

The authors and editor

Vitus Asaga Bawa is a trans-medium entertainer who has recently launched a flagship pay as you go record label called National Entertainers Union, "NEU", to enable independent art in Leeds. He is also a self employed fundraiser for charitable causes and SMEs in service of the third sector economy.

Elizabeth Bee currently works for the Adoption Register for England. She trained in Leeds both as teacher and later as a librarian and has worked in the voluntary sector for over thirty years. She has been a Liberal and Liberal Democrat candidate as well as an agent and organiser. She edits and publishes under the Beecroft imprint.

Joanne Binns is founder of the Forgotten Children's Foundation, fighting anti-social behaviour, giving care to child victims who find themselves in situations and experiences that no child should have to face and giving them an alternative in life. She is on the executive committee of Leeds East North East Liberal Democrats and has also been a Liberal Democrat City Council candidate.

Richard Brett was Councillor for Burmantofts and Richmond Hill Ward from 2004 to 2011. He was the first "Children's lead member" to take overall responsibility for all children's issues in Leeds and was leader of the Liberal Democrat Group and joint Leader of Leeds City Council from 2007 to 2010 in a coalition with the Conservatives. He is Chair of the party's English Candidate's Committee.

Ryk Downes is a Liberal Democrat councillor for Otley and Yeadon. He is Deputy Leader of the Leeds Liberal Democrat Council Group. He is Liberal Democrat leader on, and the former chair of, Metro, the West Yorkshire Integrated Transport Authority. He is the party's spokesperson for Transport. He serves on the Leeds City Council Licensing Committee. He is a Governor at Rufford Park and Ashfield Schools and a foundation governor at Prince Henry Grammar School

Dr Anthony Lockett is a consultant with over 25 years experience in the pharmaceutical industry with international clients. He is currently consulting as chief medical officer at a well established pharmaceutical company, reviewing current strategy, managing their organisational change and developing new drug pathways. Other clients have included the Department of Health. He has been a lecturer on microbiology and immunology at the London School of Tropical Medicine and has published a number of research papers. In 2013, he received a University of Strathclyde Glasgow Enterprise award.

Ian MacFadyen is a consultant and a coach. He is a former public servant. He is an associate of Teesside University Business School. He is Chair of Leeds East North East Liberal Democrats local party for 2014.

Michael Meadowcroft first joined the Liberal Party in 1958. He was elected to the Leeds City Council with two colleagues in 1968 – the first Liberals elected for 30 years – and was Leader of the Liberal Group until 1981. He was MP for Leeds West 1983-87. He has written widely on Liberal politics and his archive is available on www.bramley.demon.co.uk. In the past 25 years he has led or been a member of over 50 electoral or parliamentary missions to 36 emerging democracies.

Ruth Péchèr lives in Bramley with her husband and four children. She attended schools in Bramley and Wortley and obtained her degree in European Studies at Cardiff University. She did her teaching certificate and her Master's degree at Leeds University. She has taught for some years in inner city schools in Leeds and Bradford. She was the Liberal Democrat candidate for Armley in 2011.

APPENDIX 2

Further reading

Liberal philosophy and thinking
Dictionary of Liberal Thought
ed. Duncan Brack and Ed Randall
pub. Politico's, 2007
ISBN 978-1842751671

*Freedom, Liberty and Fairness –
Liberal Democrat Values for the
21st Century*
pub. Beecroft Publications, 2013
ISBN 978-0952702580

*An Intelligent Person's Guide to
Liberalism*
by Conrad Russell
pub. Duckworth, 1999
ISBN 978-0715629475

The Liberal Moment
by Nick Clegg
pub. Demos, 2009
ISBN 978-1906693244
www.demos.co.uk/publications/

*The Orange Book: Reclaiming
Liberalism*
ed. Paul Marshall and David Laws
pub. Profile Books 2004

ISBN 978-1861977977

*Reinventing the State – Social
Liberalism for the 21st Century*
ed. Duncan Brack, Richard
Grayson and David Howarth
pub. Politicos, 2007
ISBN 978-1842752180

Applying Liberalism
After Social Democracy
by Ralf Dahrendorf
pub. Unservile State Papers, 1980
ISBN 978-0900520846

Diversity in Danger
by Michael Meadowcroft
pub. Beecroft Publications, 2010
ISBN 978-0952702559

The Future of Politics
by Charles Kennedy
pub. HarperCollins, 2000
ISBN 978-0007101313

*The Future Tasks of Liberalism: A
Political Agenda*
by Ralf Dahrendorf

pub. John Stuart Mill Institute, 1989
ISBN 978-1871952018

Life Chances
by Ralf Dahrendorf
pub. Weidenfield & Nicholson, 1979
ISBN 978-0226134086

*The Little Yellow Book: Reclaiming
the Liberal Democrats for the People*
ed. Robert Brown and Nigel Lindsay
pub. Upfront Publishing, 2012
ISBN 978-1780352664

The Politics of Electoral Reform
by Michael Meadowcroft
pub. Electoral Reform Society, 2015

*Unlocking Liberalism – Life after
the Coalition*
ed. Robert Brown, Gillian Gloyer
and Nigel Lindsay
pub. Fastprint Publishing, 2014
ISBN 978-1784560911

Liberal History
A Dictionary of Liberal Biography
ed. Duncan Brack et al
pub. Politico's 1998
ISBN 978-1902301099

A History of the Liberal Party
by David Dutton
pub. Palgrave Macmillan, 2013
ISBN 978-0230361898

*Mothers of Liberty – Women who
built British Liberalism*
pub. Liberal Democrat History
Group, 2012

Peace, Reform and Liberation
ed. Robert Ingham & Duncan Brack
pub. Biteback Publishing, 2011
ISBN 978-1849540438

Liberal & Liberal Democrat Policy
*Change that works for you:
Building a Fairer Britain, Liberal
Democrat Manifesto, 2010*
pub. The Liberal Democrats
www.general-election-2010.co.uk/
liberal-democrat-party-manifesto-
2010-general-election

*The Coalition: our programme for
government*
pub. HM Government, 2010

Reference
The Dictionary of Liberal Quotations
ed. Duncan Brack
pub. Biteback Publishing, 2013
ISBN 978-1849545389

Online
Liberal Democrat voice -Blog
www.libdemvoice.org/

Liberal Values for a New Decade (1980)
*Social Democracy - Barrier or
Bridge?* (1981)
Liberalism and the Left (1982)
Liberalism and the Right (1983)
All by Michael Meadowcroft from:
www.bramley.demon.co.uk

Magazine
Liberator (monthly)
Subscribe via the website: www.
liberatormagazine.org.uk